MARCEL PROUST

AND

THE STRATEGY OF READING

PURDUE UNIVERSITY MONOGRAPHS
IN ROMANCE LANGUAGES

William M. Whitby, General Editor
Allan H. Pasco, Editor for French
Enrique Caracciolo-Trejo, Editor for Spanish

Associate Editors

I. French

Max Aprile, Purdue University
Paul Benhamou, Purdue University
Gerard J. Brault, Pennsylvania State University
Germaine Brée, Wake Forest University
Jules Brody, Harvard University
Victor Brombert, Princeton University
Gerald Herman, University of California, Davis
Michael Issacharoff, University of Western Ontario
Thomas E. Kelly, Purdue University
Milorad R. Margitić, Wake Forest University
Bruce A. Morrissette, University of Chicago
Robert J. Niess, Duke University
Glyn P. Norton, Pennsylvania State University
David Lee Rubin, University of Virginia
Murray Sachs, Brandeis University
English Showalter, Jr., Rutgers University, Camden
Donald Stone, Jr., Harvard University

II. Spanish

J. B. Avalle-Arce, University of North Carolina
Rica Brown, M.A., Oxon
Frank P. Casa, University of Michigan
Alan D. Deyermond, Princeton University and Westfield College (University of London)
David T. Gies, University of Virginia
Roberto González Echevarría, Yale University
Thomas R. Hart, University of Oregon
Djelal Kadir II, Purdue University
John W. Kronik, Cornell University
Floyd F. Merrell, Purdue University
Geoffrey Ribbans, Brown University
Elias L. Rivers, SUNY, Stony Brook
Francisco Ruiz Ramón, Purdue University
Bruce W. Wardropper, Duke University

Volume 4
Walter Kasell
*Marcel Proust and
the Strategy of Reading*

WALTER KASELL

MARCEL PROUST

AND

THE STRATEGY OF READING

AMSTERDAM / JOHN BENJAMINS B. V.

1980

© Copyright 1980 — John Benjamins B.V.
ISBN 90 272 1714 9

No part of this book may be reproduced in any form, by print, photoprint, microfilm or any other means, without written permission from the publisher.

for my children, Jacob and Miriam

Table of Contents

Abbreviations . . . . *viii*

Acknowledgments . . . . *ix*

Introduction. 1

1. The Pilgrimage: Proust Reads Ruskin 18

2. The Magic Voyage: Proust Reads Nerval 31

3. The Reader as Judge 45

4. The Textuality of Albertine 60

5. Marcel's Fictional Project: A Strategy of Recovery 81

6. Conclusion: The Narrative Implications. 98

Notes 111

Bibliography. 119

Abbreviations

Works by Marcel Proust commonly referred to in the text:

A la recherche du temps perdu. Edited and presented by Pierre Clarac and André Ferré. 3 vols. Bibliothèque de la Pléiade. Paris: Gallimard, 1954. Indicated in the text by volume and page number in parentheses.

Contre Sainte-Beuve: précédé de Pastiches et mélanges et suivi de Essais et articles. Edited by Pierre Clarac and Yves Sandre. Bibliothèque de la Pléiade. Paris: Gallimard, 1971. Indicated by *CSB*.

Jean Santeuil précédé de Les Plaisirs et les jours. Edited by Pierre Clarac and Yves Sandre. Bibliothèque de la Pléiade. Paris: Gallimard, 1971. Indicated by *JS*.

Acknowledgments

I would like to thank Librairie Gallimard for permission to quote from the Pléiade editions of Proust's works. The chapter on Proust and Ruskin has appeared in somewhat different form in *La Revue de littérature comparée*, 44, No. 4 (Oct.-Dec. 1975), 547-60, and the chapter on Proust and Nerval, in *Romanic Review*, 68, No. 3, (May 1977), 165-74, and I am grateful to those journals for permission to reprint that material.

Much of this work was done as a Humboldt Fellow at the University of Constance, for which opportunity I thank the Alexander von Humboldt Foundation. Support has also been given to this project by Brandeis University and Princeton University.

I wish to thank all my teachers and friends of the past few years, who have enhanced and brightened my study of literature. Special thanks are due to Profs. Paul de Man and Neil Hertz, who assisted me in my dissertation on Proust, to David Grossvogel, whose graduate seminar introduced me to Proust's novel, and to Wolfgang Holdheim, who generously read portions of my work in its early stages. Since then, I am most grateful for the encouragement which I received from many colleagues and teachers, especially Hans-Robert Jauss and Walter Strauss, Wolfgang Iser and Germaine Brée. Allan Pasco has been exceptionally helpful in the preparation of this manuscript for publication. And last, but certainly not least, my wife, Eva, who has been most patient and supportive at all times.

Introduction

> *La configuration d'une chose n'est pas seulement l'image de sa nature, c'est le mot de sa destinée et le tracé de son histoire.*
>
> —Marcel Proust

One does not approach lightly *A la recherche du temps perdu*. Words of analysis must be added carefully to the thousands of pages of the novel and the many books of criticism. Neither does this study claim to offer a "total" reading of Proust's monumental novel; it does, however, try to refocus the general critical approach to that work. In so doing, it hopes to join a recent movement of readjustment, a rereading of the *Recherche* which has been occurring for the past fifteen years in the works of Marcel Muller, Gilles Deleuze, Paul de Man, and Gérard Genette. These critics have helped to recast the terms of the dialogue readers have been engaging in since *A la recherche du temps perdu* first appeared in 1913.

By beginning with an examination of Proust's early critical essays, seen as attempts to learn about the nature of fiction, I try deliberately to question the traditional, progressive reading of the novel. Such a reading is crucially inadequate, since it ultimately depends on taking the narrator at his word and accepting his explanations and claims *in place of* the actual experience of reading the novel. Every work of fiction tends to claim a unified totality, perceived and expressed in a privileged voice, and *A la recherche du temps perdu* is no exception. Especially toward the end of the novel, Proust's narrator tries to privilege his own perspective and name the terms in which the narrative has succeeded. As one critic noted, "the evidence suggests rather, that although Proust meant to show us that the young Marcel's judgments were naive and false, he was quite serious about the validity of the older Marcel's 'laws.' "[1] It will be my task to show how the assertions of this voice are undermined by the rest of the text. To do this, it will be necessary to perceive the irreducible complexity of the narrative and show to what extent the *Recherche* is *not* an easy or a comfortable text, but one founded on a disequilibrium.

The opening of the novel finds the narrator trying to situate himself in his room, in time, and in the limbo of consciousness between sleep and wakefulness. His uncertain movement among the possibilities that occur to him holds definite orientation in abeyance—an uncertainty imparted to the reader by the syntactic ambiguity of the novel's first sentence: "Longtemps je me suis couché de bonne heure." The adverb of time seems to call for a verb in the imperfect to indicate a repeated action in the past, but it receives the perfective form. At the very outset then, an unresolvable disjunction appears in the language of this novel. Incompatible statements or directions are deliberately juxtaposed to form a new, yet uncomfortably puzzling whole: the similarity of reading to the temporal and physical dislocation the narrator feels is intimated by the very first words of the novel. The comfort of knowing for sure where one stands is withdrawn at the moment of the text's inception—if it was ever really available in the first place. It is at once made clear that the reading of Proust's novel will be inseparable from a lesson in reading and a continual demonstration of the complexity and elusiveness of the fictional text.

Reading, seen first as a theme in Proust's work, then in its implications for the structure of *A la recherche du temps perdu*, is the subject of this study. It begins with the group of essays on John Ruskin, written while Proust was translating two books by his English mentor, *The Bible of Amiens* and *Sesame and Lilies*. One essay, which will serve as a preface to one of the translations, is even entitled "Sur la lecture"; it examines reading as an activity and as a structuring of experience. I wish to focus on a text where Proust catches himself reading Ruskin, in his words, "idolatrously," and I will follow the notion of "idolatry," the ability of a text to deceive the reader (or writer) through language, into Proust's essays on Nerval and Sainte-Beuve. An analogy will be developed between Marcel's various projects in the *Recherche*—his attempt to enter society, to capture Albertine, to travel to the Venice or the Balbec of his dreams, or to reach his vocation—and a reader's attempt to seize the essence of a text and appropriate it. In light of this comparison, it will finally become possible to locate the "strategy" of the narrative.

As the narrative quickly establishes, reading is an experience of radical disorientation where the text presents several directions at once. The reader, who is searching for a single, certain direction to follow and who, like the narrator, would locate himself firmly with respect to the text, finds himself thrown between too many possible "certainties." Like Albertine, the text is always too much for the reader: never reducible to its literal level nor liberated completely from that literal dimension, it lies always in between these poles. The writer struggles with language, trying to overcome language's unavoidable concreteness, to declare his—and his language's—independence. His ideal language would assert the complete investment of only his poetic intention. He must forever discover, however, an inevitable remainder, evidence of the impossibility of avoiding the meanings and overtones which preexist in his language or which express an unintentional presence in his projects. His text is always revealing language's ability to go beyond his intentions; the text is in fact constituted by several sets of movements which interact in a kind of counterpoint. As his opening page indicates, Proust is interested in the moment of transition, from sleep to waking or from the book to real life. The points in the text to be examined here are often those carefully located in between the possible fixed points of reference, where language seems to juxtapose incompatible elements, as in a pun. In those moments, the text refutes its own literality, even while it cannot free itself from concreteness. Proust locates his fiction between poles of singular, "univalent" orientation, between its literal and figurative elements, between its apparent intention and the excesses of language.

In the essays on Ruskin, Proust is watching himself in the act of reading. The manner in which he turns this experience into an "allegory" of reading suggests a strategy later to be written into the *Recherche*. The set of concerns established in those essays will suggest how Proust's conception of the reading experience structures his text. My reading will try to insist always on the multiplicity of directions in the narrative and, especially, on the evidence that continually argues against simple acceptance of Marcel's steady progress. Even the use of the name "Marcel" for the narrator may be seen as yet another aspect of the novel's attempt to dislocate the apparent origin of the text.[2] From the text's refusal to admit one single, privileged meaning, the entire movement of the narrator's progress toward his vocation may be called into question. Throughout the work, the great difficulty—for reader, narrator, and characters alike—of seeing clearly or judging with certainty qualifies the narrator's attempts to appropriate his world. Nevertheless, a project may be discerned which tries to use these very limitations in order to transcend them.

Since the narrator's explicit pronouncements are suspect, it is essential to pursue an indirect path through this textual labyrinth. As Paul de Man has noted at the beginning of his important essay on Proust and reading, "il s'agit précisément de savoir si ce dont il est question dans un texte littéraire correspond à ce qui s'y trouve énoncé."[3] Proust's metaphors for his novel, such as the cathedral, are well known; however, images of Marcel's novelistic project, while less striking, may offer greater insight into the strategy of *A la recherche du temps perdu*. We find one such image in a passage appropriately located between two clear portions of the novel, between his introduction to the "côté de Méséglise" and the "côté de Guermantes." Marcel recalls there an unusual fishing expedition and offers an image whose structure describes the literary project on which he is about to embark. He has come to the Vivonne to escape the disorder of Easter preparations at his aunt's, to the river "qui se promenait déjà en bleu ciel entre les terres encore noires et nues."[4] The narrator remembers that while watching some young boys trying to catch fish in bottles suspended in the rushing stream, he experienced an image of exhilarating freshness:

> Je m'amusais à regarder les carafes que les gamins mettaient dans la Vivonne pour prendre les petits poissons, et qui, remplies par la rivière où elles sont à leur tour encloses, à la fois "contenant" aux flancs transparents comme une eau durcie et "contenu" plongé dans un plus grand contenant de cristal liquide et courant, évoquaient l'image de la fraîcheur d'une façon plus délicieuse et plus irritante qu'elles n'eussent fait sur une table servie, en ne la montrant qu'en fuite dans cette allitération perpétuelle entre l'eau sans consistance où les mains ne pouvaient la capter et le verre sans fluidité où le palais ne pourrait en jouir. (I, 168)

For a number of reasons, this passage has attracted considerable attention recently, although no one has specifically insisted on it as an image of Marcel's writing project.[5] And although the hidden theme of the fisherman is already linked to that project, what attracts Marcel's attention here has little to do with the fish the boys may catch. The intentions of these fishermen are quickly superseded by the deliciously irritating sensation the scene provokes:

> Je me promettais de venir là plus tard avec des lignes; j'obtenais qu'on tirât un peu de pain des provisions du goûter, j'en jetais dans la Vivonne des boulettes qui semblaient suffire pour y provoquer un phénomène de sursaturation, car l'eau se solidifiait aussitôt autour d'elles en grappes ovoïdes de têtards inanitiés qu'elle tenait sans doute jusque-là en dissolution, invisibles, tout près d'être en voie de cristallisation. (I, 168)

In a sense, the scene offers a microcosm of the narrative as a whole: Marcel enters the way he begins the novel, as an observer, and leaves as he will at the end, promising to become an active participant, returning "avec des lignes." The passage occurs in a context of aesthetic pleasure which the narrator cannot consummate by appropriation. He has just examined some flowers whose "visage incompréhensible" seemed the more brilliant because they defied his attempt to seize them: "Jaunes come un jaune d'œuf, brillant d'autant plus, me semblait-il, que ne pouvant dériver vers aucune velléité de dégustation le plaisir que leur vue me causait . . ." (I, 167-68). Here too, Marcel is faced with a deliciously elusive quality. Suspended in the stream, the bottles situate themselves between the flow of the river and the "captured" water they contain. The stream and carafes exchange their respective properties, the bottles becoming a kind of "eau durcie," while the river surrounding them becomes a great flowing vessel of "cristal liquide."

Marcel's image initiates a play of container and contents, much like a novel which creates the world in which it is itself contained. By virtue of their intermediate position, the bottles divide the water into two different "forms," whose juxtaposition in turn creates an image of "fraîcheur" far more striking than that which the water alone could produce. The delicious irritation that Marcel feels in response to the image will be shown to be an exemplary Proustian reaction. It is elicited by a certain irreducible complexity, the "perpetual alliteration" between the flowing water, desirable because it cannot be seized, and the "eau durcie," hardened and captured beyond the possibility of enjoyment. The image has captured his attention between two "negative" elements, the "eau sans consistance" and the "verre sans fluidité." The carafes which separate the two waters, through their transparency, are able to transcend this difference and resemble, in this respect, the language which creates the image of inaccessibility.

The "fraîcheur en fuite" that the narrator describes is the product of a rhetorical *tour de force*, of what Gérard Genette has called an "exchange of predicates."[6] The two elements in Marcel's image combine into a new and complex unity, in which it suddenly seems possible to capture the movement of *fraîcheur*. The rhetorical figure has introduced a new "ground" of possibility, in which the elusive flow can be seized. *Within the image*, it appears to Marcel that he can capture, and savor materially, the delicious flowing water. Later, in more elaborate forms of the same project, he will attempt to possess physically the woman who charms him from a distance. Such attempts reveal the force and attraction of metaphor, for the possibility of seizing the *fraîcheur* exists only on the level of language. In fact, by creating such an illusion, making the water seem to capture itself, this becomes an image of metaphor itself. If Marcel is to return successfully to this scene, "avec des lignes," he will have to engage in a literary project, not a sporting one. His principal error through this novel of quest will be to try to enact this capture on the level of reality. But the temptation to transfer to reality the possibilities language has opened up, itself expresses the seductive—and deceptive—nature of the image.

A new space is created by this juxtaposition of incompatible elements, a "middle distance" between them, within which the activity of fiction can take place. It is essential to realize that the exchange of predicates is *constantly occurring*, making the text itself a "perpetual alliteration" of interchange which maintains the ground of fiction by preserving the tension in which it can exist. The language of fiction continually generates the play between similitude and difference, re-creating the transformation which forms the image. Simile, as Coleridge once said, never runs on four feet; it establishes itself and exists, rather, in the tension between the identity toward which it is moving and the difference, increasingly apparent as the tenor approaches its vehicle. The narrator's image here is structured by the continued presence of two opposing movements, a structure whose implications we will want to explore in the chapters that follow. In the final, grand novel, it will be possible to rediscover in Marcel what Proust found in examining his own reading of Ruskin: that truth lies along the path of error, and corruption at the heart of purity. Yet these moments must be seen as necessary complements, invariably co-present, and constantly being transformed into one another. Proust's transparent carafes offer the reader an image of identity which is simultaneous with the difference it is always in the process of overcoming. Linguists distinguish between language as *system*, determined by the correlation "either–or," and as *process*, where language is determined by the relation "both–and."[7] The poetic text, however, manages to be both a process of transformation and a product of that process.

Writing is not merely the result of such complex activity, but its continual enactment. Certain texts, as Edward Said has shown in his brilliant rereading of Freud, enact themselves in order, like the dream itself, to deny the priority of any potentially "anterior" texts:

> The novel most explicitly realizes these [textual] conventions, gives them coherence and imaginative life by grounding them in a text whose beginning premise is, as we have said above, paternal. This is decidedly not the case with Freud's writing ... [8]

For this "paternal" relation of chronological succession, Said finds, Freud's text substitutes "brothers for fathers, co-presence for consecutiveness, temporal and spatial simultaneity for the (relative) finality of sequence."[9] In similar fashion, Proust's text enacts itself in order to deny a privileged status to any single position reached at one point or another along the novel's itinerary. This is not an easy attitude to maintain, but the image of the carafes in the Vivonne gives a certain insight into the text as both process and product. In a narrative, as in an image, that process must be seen as preserving its untransformed elements, as well as its final result. The narrative describes this movement of transformation diachronically, but the metaphor preserves the history of its formation in what I call a *constellation* of its elements. As Paul de Man has recognized, there is an important complementarity of the synchronic and diachronic dimensions in Proust's text:

> Le moment et le récit seraient complémentaires et symétriques, reflets spéculaires qui pourraient se remplacer sans laisser de résidu. Par un acte de mémoire ou d'anticipation, le récit se substitue à l'expérience comme la lecture se substitue au récit.[10]

De Man situates the quality of *fraîcheur* in Proust, however, entirely along the pole of interiority, as "l'un des attributs caractéristiques du monde dit intérieur."[11] If we trace Proust's sense of that term back to his essays on Ruskin, it becomes clear that the peculiar *fraîcheur* of fiction is constituted, rather, by the troubling juxtaposition of incongruent planes. It grows out of a response to the ability of language to be both "interior" and "exterior." The diverse, even contradictory forms *en fuite*, changing into one another, will be present at once, like the figures which Marcel notices in Giotto's painting. The *fraîcheur* expresses his reaction, at one point, to the divergent, simultaneous images evoked by the city-name Florence:

> [C]omme certains tableaux de Giotto eux-mêmes qui montrent à deux moments différents de l'action un même personnage, ici couché dans son lit, là s'apprêtant à monter à cheval, le nom de Florence était-il divisé en deux compartiments. (I, 389-90)

In the image's action of transformation, and in the process of containing and being contained, the elements of the image exist *both* "à leur tour" *and* "à la fois." Any notion of real progress is suspended by this constellation, as the "earlier," untransformed aspects of the process are present in the "later," impossible water. The interaction of the image's elements is a constant activity, an "allitération perpétuelle," which requires the co-presence of each element, and between these poles the movement of interpenetration establishes and maintains the space of fiction.

Proust seems to feel that meaning, like the essence of any creative work, must be fashioned by the reader at a virtual point "in between" the poles of meaning offered by the text. In an early essay, Proust suggests that the real genius of a painter lies in between his individual works:

> Ce qu'il y a dans un tableau d'un peintre ne peut pas nourrir [son esprit], ni dans un livre d'un auteur non plus, et dans un second tableau du peintre, un second livre d'un auteur. Mais si dans le second tableau ou le second livre, il aperçoit quelque chose qui n'est pas dans le second et dans le premier, mais qui en quelque sorte est entre les deux, dans une sorte de tableau idéal, qu'il voit en matière spirituelle se modeler hors du tableau, il a reçu sa nourriture et recommence à exister et à être heureux.[12]

Genius must be grasped on its own special grounds, between the whole and the detail, "car il meurt instantanément dans le particulier, et se remet à flotter et à vivre dans le général" (*CSB*, p. 304). Proust, here, is echoing the Romantic conviction that, although poetry seems to fulfill and "lose" itself in its concrete representation, it never allows itself to be reduced to any single manifestation.[13] He seems also to express the desire to free his language from the limitations of the empirical world. He would liberate it from its material form and establish its independence as purely figurative language. It is indicative that Proust returns several times in his writings to Flaubert's description of reality as merely "pour l'emploi d'une illusion à décrire."[14] When Marcel vows to return "avec des lignes," he is dreaming of a language which, like the image of the carafes, can maintain the contradictions it creates. Such a language would always remain in the tension "between" fixed points of meaning, containing itself and yet producing the flow within which it is contained.

Such a project sounds like a mad poet's dream, but it clearly anticipates the novel which tells the story of its own genesis. As Edward Said expressed it,

> [Proust's] text is polymorphous to the extent that it includes not only the career of the writer who (might have) produced it, but also his life before he was a producer and a description of its putative genesis.[15]

In his short but important essay on Gérard de Nerval, Proust emphasizes the essential connection between Nerval's complex fiction and his recurring bouts of madness. He discovers in the narrative itself traces of Nerval's surrender to his fantasies, which culminated in his inability to distinguish them from reality. The middle distance that Nerval created as an artist eventually swallowed him up, but what most interested Proust was the quality of the narrative as it approached that unresolvable complexity. He found Nerval's madness an extreme form of the attitude toward reality that he had already seen in Flaubert. But although reality may be a mere pretext, an "illusion" from which the text borrows its subject matter, it is a pretext from which the writer—and his language—never wholly escape. Proust locates Nerval's power in the lengths to which he took this project as well as in his ability to situate his text always on the edge of a kind of "insanity," portraying, finally, the fundamental nature of all fictional language.

The text's refusal to conform to one definite meaning necessitates constant redefinition: all along the way, the reader must be revising his sense of the situation. His similarity to the narrator's position makes it possible to talk of Marcel's "reading" his world.[16] In the dimension of characters, someone like Charlus will have to be reinterpreted numerous times, perhaps endlessly, while on the rhetorical level, the narrative overwhelms the notion of identity altogether, presenting objects in a continual metamorphosis, a proliferation of analogies and metaphors. And syntactically, the middle ground is maintained by Proust's intricate sentences which, like those of Saint-Simon, "against all expectation" deliberately resist finding their resolution where the reader anticipates it. Such tactics move the reader away from certainty and orientation. The *fraîcheur* Marcel feels, and which Proust once called "ce trouble délicieux" (*CSB*, p. 240), arises as a response to juxtaposed forms of reality, the troubled overtones of guilt recalling an "idolatrous" violation of the text. The peculiar simultaneity of language, created by its ability to operate as fiction *and* as reality, literally referential *and* figuratively connotative, makes it seem possible to the reader to contain the image's *fraîcheur*, or to travel in reality to the "pays de Sylvie." In *A la recherche du temps perdu*, this intermediary position often expresses Marcel's desire to have things both ways, that is, to possess his ideal in real form. Throughout the novel, much of his search is for the particular person who can embody in herself all the potential his imagination has invested in her. Marcel would possess in the flesh the girl seen from afar, "balancée par mon imagination," as he describes it, "devant l'horizon marin" (II, 351-52). At one point, Proust called "sincerity" this desire to actualize an imaginary reality, not in order to indicate a moral quality, but to describe the serious conviction that one can cross the fictional distance. And he created the character Marcel, part of whose project is to try to locate himself at the point where choices have not yet been made and all possibilities are still available.[17] In counterpoint to the "trouble délicieux," however, we should not overlook Marcel's (and Proust's) sense that none of these pleasures is "pure" and that all are troubled by a hidden "idolatry," a concept Proust elaborates in his essay on Ruskin. Our later discussion of *A la recherche* focuses on the textual strategy which places the reader in a similar position, tempting him to read the work literally in the belief that Marcel's progress shows the way out of the textual labyrinth.

These movements of the text indicate a structure of transformation in which the various stages of the process persist and continue to interact. This phenomenon is what caused Gérard Genette to call Proust's work a "palimpseste," in which no elements or variants may be completely disregarded:

> Comme l'écriture proustienne, l'œuvre de Proust est un palimpseste où se confondent et s'enchevêtrent plusieurs sens, toujours présents tous à la fois, et qui ne se laissent déchiffrer que tous ensemble, dans leur inextricable totalité.[18]

The constellation of different "moments" in a development describes a dialectic of nonexclusive alternatives, and forms an essential part of the novel's strategy. Progress, which is the apparent mode of production of both texts and metaphors, cannot fully describe their dynamic construction, for unchanged and partially transformed elements remain inscribed in the history of that production. The image and its elements form a *triadic* relationship: they stand in a dynamic and continual, but essentially nonlinear, relation to one another, a link in which "its three members are bound together by it in a way that does not consist of any complexus of diadic relations."[19] That is, at no time may any one aspect of the text be said to comprehend or transcend the others, but always relates to them multivalently.

A perception of such a narrative structure will show how Proust's novel is characterized by a fundamental ambivalence calculated to put in question the narrator's organization of his own experience. Although Marcel can be seen progressing toward a clear understanding of himself and his world, its codes, its structure and his place in it, his vocation, yet this movement is undermined by countercurrents in the narrative which demand a constant reevaluation of the hero's apparent progress. Once we have examined the Proustian problematic of reading and the narrative strategies discovered in the early essays, we will be able to point out aspects of the *Recherche* which call into question the entire possibility of appropriating a clear vision

10   Proust's Strategy of Reading

of the world. Marcel, we notice, wants to authenticate his image of the world: already in *Combray* he reveals the need to *realize* his vision by seizing it in its undeniable and physical particularity in the real world. Like Nerval, he will travel to the place of the woman, and like Swann, he will refuse to "cheat desire" by substituting an easy conquest for the woman actually desired. In order for an experience to be *real* for Marcel, it must be consummated by the unique figure that inspired it. The girl who he imagines will offer him the essence of the Roussainville countryside is crucially irreplaceable:

> J'avais le désir d'une paysanne de Méséglise ou de Roussainville, d'une pécheuse de Balbec, comme j'avais le désir de Méséglise et de Balbec. Le plaisir qu'elles pouvaient me donner m'aurait paru moins vrai, je n'aurais plus cru en lui, si j'en avais modifié à ma guise les conditions. Connaître à Paris une pêcheuse de Balbec ou une paysanne de Méséglise, c'eût été recevoir des coquillages que je n'aurais pas vus sur la plage . . . . (I, 157)

The peasant girl he fantasizes is linked genuinely to the land like the Guermantes and has, in this way, been invested by Marcel's imagination with the secret genius of that landscape. She represents a perfect conjunction of his imagination and the irrefutable "otherness" of the real, at once objectifying his fantasy and authenticating it. By this harmonization of self and other, she will yield to him the penetration into the real which he has failed to achieve by contemplating merely the landscape itself. She will be a supplement to the hawthorns which resist him:

> Mais errer ainsi dans les bois de Roussainville sans une paysanne à embrasser, c'était ne pas connaître de ces bois le trésor caché, la beauté profonde. Cette fille que je ne voyais que criblée de feuillages, elle était elle-même pour moi comme une plante locale d'une espèce plus élevée seulement que les autres et dont la structure permet d'approcher de plus près qu'en elles la saveur profonde du pays. (I, 157)

This project is of course thwarted, as is the parallel project on the level of language. Marcel is frustrated in addressing the woman he loves by the suspicion that the terms he uses do not depend on her, but will reemerge in subsequent affairs. Increasingly throughout the novel, the attempt at authentification reveals itself as a subtle form of idolatry, an error of reading that transposes the image from the rhetorical level to that of empirical reality.

The structure of nonexclusive alternatives tries to take the dynamics of the fictional narrative beyond a sense of transformation in which elements "progress" by leaving their history behind them and discarding the "early stages." Proust's novel is in many ways the story of error, and as such cannot sustain a reading which effaces the traces of that error's commission. The critic who finds, in describing the various movements of Proust's narrative, that one of them "n'est qu'un mouvement illusoire" reveals that this "erroneous" dimension does not exist meaningfully for him. Within this logic, when the movement of error is superseded by truth, the transcended error is annulled:

> Lorsque le second mouvement (celui qui est orienté vers la recherche de l'œuvre) reçoit son objet, il annule le premier mouvement (la recherche d'un bien de la vie).[20]

The inadequacy of the logic of exclusion for the reading of a literary text recalls the observation that most double entendres are really singular in their meaning. But the text of the *Recherche* is formed by a simultaneous weaving and unweaving that Walter Benjamin called a "Penelope-work of remembrance,"[21] a process demanding a reading that acknowledges the constant co-presence of its several movements. The textual structure has been built to inspire—yet also to resist the urge toward a reductive resolution. Theses being fashioned on one level for Marcel (and for the reader) are frequently being deconstructed on other levels. In the text, as in Marcel's mind as he hesitates between courses of action, both alternatives are "true":

> Dans un autre sens aussi, les deux tendances, dans l'espèce celle qui me faisait tenir à ce que ma lettre partît, et, quand je la croyais partie, à le regretter, ont l'une et l'autre en elles leur vérité. (III, 460)

This insistence on the presence of several directions of movement in the text is an appeal for appreciation of the profound complexity of the *Recherche*. In the discussion that follows, I will be arguing that Marcel's apparent "progress" is not the object of a privileged perspective, but must be read in the context of evidence indicating that error is constitutive of Marcel's world, and sound judgement a dubious possibility. The numerous directions ceaselessly interacting to form this narrative suggest a text whose *nature* is labyrinthine, and the reading of which demands a sense of their interplay at every point. One can distinguish, for example, as Roland Barthes does, between the "decoding" movement of the text ("Marcel") and "Proust," the name we can give to the movement of "encoding."[22] Marcel, who is always trying to find his way through the complexity of language and experience he encounters, expresses the problematic situation of one who must interpret and judge signs. For "Proust," however, the problem is not one of deciphering his world, but of finding a structure and language for his novel. Nevertheless, there is an irresistible urge to have the two coincide; there is an invitation in the text itself to read it *à la lettre*, collapsing the triadic structure, or as Paul de Man has indicated in a temporal framework, to close off the dynamic interaction between the text's constitutive directions:

12   Proust's Strategy of Reading

> La forme littéraire résulte de cette combinaison dialectique de la préfiguration avec la notion de totalité interprétative. Cette dialectique est difficile à saisir. L'idée de totalité suggère des structures closes, qui ont une tendance presque irrésistible à se laisser transformer en structures objectives. Pourtant, l'élément temporel, sans cesse oublié, devrait nous rappeler que la forme n'est jamais qu'un processus en route vers sa totalisation.[23]

One characteristic problem for readers of the *Recherche* is the tendency to read the text biographically, identifying the character as the author. André Maurois, whose *A la recherche de Marcel Proust* already confuses in its title the writer and his work, begins by effortlessly merging Proust's *story* with his personal history: "L'histoire de Marcel Proust est, comme le décrit son livre, celle d'un homme qui a tendrement aimé le monde de son enfance."[24] Of course, most readers would now avoid this grosser error and agree that, regardless of whether or not Proust tenderly loved the world of his childhood, his life is not "comme le décrit son livre." Yet on another level, the text seems constantly to invite us to be led by Marcel through the novel, taking him at his word and accepting his explanations as privileged, that is, as though they were spoken directly by the author. This temptation is especially strong in the final volume of the *Recherche*, where Marcel finally appears to reach his vocation and offer a clear explanation of how he has arrived there—almost as though admitting these insights were not available from the preceding narration. Proust seems at last to drop the role of Marcel here and to speak out in his own voice. Indeed, too many critics rely, for the substantiation of their reading of Proust, on the deceptively clear theoretical pronouncements of *Le Temps retrouvé*. In so doing, they betray their readiness to come away from the site of the text— an evasion which Proust knew well and which he exposed in his earliest critical essays. Such readings circumvent the complexity of the text by eliminating its key structural element, the narrative voice as its apparent origin. These readers would have the author, representing the true and unique origin of the work, offer its genuine meaning directly. Yet the simplicity they discover is itself deceptive, for nowhere perhaps is the voice "Marcel" better characterized by his *struggle* to become "Proust" than in that last book. He need not succeed in that attempt, of course, no more than the poet who seeks to liberate his text from the "illusion" of reality—although Proust would surely have us believe Marcel succeeds. But there are several voices that weave the text of the *Recherche*, a procedure to which Marcel always remains the indispensable "pretext."

Another, but less visible, form of taking Marcel at his word is the uncritical acceptance of the structure and terms in which the narrator has organized his experience. In his own account, Marcel develops steadily from a position of innocence and confusion, through a series of social, sexual, and artistic initiations, until the organization of his world and the task before him become—in his terms—*clear*. He seems at last able, by virtue of a unique experience of self-awareness, to see himself and his world clearly and to perceive his artistic task: he seems to have attained his vocation. Indeed this clarity of vision is reflected in the direct theoretical statements which fill the last two hundred pages of the novel, despite the admission that "[u]ne œuvre où il y a des théories est comme un objet sur lequel on laisse la marque du prix" (III, 882). Gaëtan Picon has described the *Recherche* as ending in a mirror: now that Marcel's life has been lived, he can begin his novel, his fictional life. In such an interpretation, the direction of the novel is simply inverted at the end: "De progressif, ce mouvement [recherche de la vie] devient régressif—non plus recherche d'un 'à vivre,' mais recherche d'un 'vécu.' "[25] These terms, however, are inadequate to describe the structure of the event. Surely Marcel experiences a sudden redefinition of his past in the last book, but the movement of the narrative, as well as the lessons of judgement and desire, show that this inversion of perspectives is not a single event, but one occurring throughout the novel. We might even go so far as to say that *A la recherche du temps perdu* is characterized by this perpetual inversion which finally deconstructs the notion of identity itself. The question remains, rather, how we are to understand that a novel so constructed seems to end in the apparent closure of the process. The strategy which suggests itself belongs neither to Proust nor to Marcel. It is a function of the text to which we must return.

The directions which appear to structure the work are not univalent but dialectical, encompassing opposing tendencies and presenting varying meanings and significances at different moments in the novel. When Jean Rousset remarks that for Marcel, "toute activité sociale est un leurre et engendre un état de mort spirituelle pour qui a vocation de créateur," he is noticing only one aspect of the experience. An interpretation which imposes a single significance on the narrator's social activity, like Picon's notion of error, reduces part of the text to something inessential. Once the illusions of the social whirl are dissipated, Rousset seems to claim, the true path of art can be pursued unhindered: "Quand cette illusion d'unité et de continuité [du monde social] se sera dissipée, la voie sera libre pour la connaissance de l'unité et de la continuité véritables."[26] Such an explanation, however, follows *Marcel's* sense of the experience, but represents only one side of the text, as though the title of the novel were not a play on "temps perdu." Even if this *is* the story of Marcel's progress, the body of the novel is an itinerary of error. And when he tells his story, taking the reader along the tortuous path he followed, it is not simply, as Rousset states, in order that the demonstration "soit convaincante," but because the experience of being captivated by the social illusion is part of Marcel's enlightenment. From the reader's perspective, the story of that "erroneous" involvement is itself a lesson in Marcel's "misreading" his world. His social activity is more than just a "leurre" and "mort spirituelle," for the time lost in the salons contains the time regained—recovered, as it were, in the material of the novel.

By accepting the structure of the narrative in the form in which it is offered, critics and readers of Proust have tended to forget that it is organized intentionally. The "progressive" movement of Marcel's apprenticeship and the approach to his vocation, however, constitute only *one* possible organization of that experience—Marcel's. His story must be read at every point as *his* interpretation, his version of the experience, for it bears everywhere the imprint of his desires, his errors, and his intentions, as well as his particular conceptions of temporality, progress, error, and the possibility of reaching a clear image of the world. It is surprising then, how many of Proust's finest critics have accepted Marcel's description of his experience without questioning its structural premises. Gilles Deleuze has organized his excellent study of Marcel's initiation into the world of signs to follow the narrator's ascent to his artistic vocation, and even Hans-Robert Jauss, in his penetrating analysis of the temporal complexity of the *Recherche* and of the crucial role of memory,[27] appears to accept the given structure of progress and ultimate success. Yet it will be possible in this study to describe a notion of history in Proust's work which tends to deny the kind of progress Marcel claims. Marcel's progress must be seen as part of his narrative intention: it is one of the ways in which the narrator wants to see himself and not a privileged and objective structure of the world. This is not to say that "nothing" happens in the Hôtel de Guermantes at the novel's end, but that the events do not necessarily conform to Marcel's claim and that they reveal perhaps far more than he intends.

The point can be illustrated by comparing the unity Proust claims for his novel with the admiration he felt for the works of Balzac and Wagner. The decisive factor for both Proust and his narrator, in their esteem for *La Comédie humaine*, is the breadth of Balzac's project—but especially the fact that its essence, the author's sense of the whole, only became apparent to Balzac after many of the individual novels had been written. That is, Balzac realized what he had accomplished only when, as author, he was sufficiently removed from his creation to enjoy the perspective Marcel calls "le regard à la fois d'un étranger et d'un père" (III, 161).[28] The authenticity of the project is guaranteed for Marcel (as for Proust) by the fact that Balzac *discovers* a unity in the works themselves, "en projetant sur eux une illumination rétrospective," rather than superimposing it from without. The whole thereby avoids the mechanical systematization which, for Marcel, comes of beginning with a set plan to which particulars have then to be made to conform:

> Unité ultérieure, non factice, sinon elle fût tombée en poussière comme tant de systématisations d'écrivains médiocres qui, à grand renfort de titres et de sous-titres, se donnent l'apparence d'avoir poursuivi un seul et transcendant dessein. Non factice, peut-être même plus réelle d'être ultérieure, d'être née d'un moment d'enthousiasme où elle est découverte entre des morceaux qui n'ont plus qu'à se rejoindre; unité qui s'ignorait, donc vitale et non logique, qui n'a pas proscrit la variété, refroidi l'exécution. (III, 161)

Introduction 15

In discussing his own novel, however, Proust defended its unity by describing a very different method of composition. Of the unquestionable rigor of its construction, he wrote to a friend, "On ne pourra la nier quand la dernière page du *Temps retrouvé* (écrit avant le reste du livre) se refermera exactement sur la première de Swann."[29] There is a clear discrepancy here between the kind of unity Proust admired in Balzac and that which he claims to have built deliberately into the *Recherche*. It is possible of course that the unity sensed by the character Marcel is of the order of that discovered by Proust in Balzac or Wagner, but this would only reveal the difference between Proust and Marcel as a function of the latter's role in the novel. Both that role and the structure of the novel are part of a larger intentional whole; it is paramount, therefore, to ask *for whom* the structures described exist. In another letter, Proust confirms that the superstructure of his novel was erected first and the rest filled in afterwards: "Le dernier chapitre du dernier volume a été écrit tout de suite après le premier chapitre du premier volume. Tout 'l'entre-deux' a été écrit ensuite."[30] The coherence of the whole seems assured thereby—until we seek the Balzacian "discovery" of harmony. "Tout 'l'entre-deux' " constitutes the entire body of the novel; this is a novel, however, much of whose activity questions the possibility of controlling the kind of neat structure which Proust postulates here—and which he disdained in the systematization of "mediocre writers." It is precisely this "entre-deux," with its mystified projects of desire and judgement, which will establish for us—often beyond Proust's evident intentions—the character of *A la recherche du temps perdu*.

Yet, in another sense, the confusion of Proust and Marcel is perhaps as inevitable as its correction, for both directions have been inscribed in the text. A look at an early Proust story may help illuminate this play of narrative movements. In "La Confession d'une jeune fille," one of the stories from his earliest collection, *Les Plaisirs et les jours* (1896), Proust organized a narrative strategy aimed at preserving an impossible vision, one whose premises are denied by the rest of the story. It is the story of a girl's sexual transgressions, whose retelling reestablishes the moment of innocence and fullness to which she is attempting to return. The sight of her promiscuity has killed her beloved mother, and in remorse, the young narrator has shot herself. In dying, and with a clear sense of her "crime," she longs to return to the scene of her childhood innocence, where she remembers receiving the full and undisguised love of her mother. "Nul lieu n'est plus plein de ma mère,"[31] she says of the park where she spent her childhood summers. But the plenitude she recalls, as the story makes clear, is a product of memory, and the narrative confession acts deliberately to postpone confrontation with this illusion. The landscape of the park, "Les Oublis," is in fact devoid of her mother's presence, for she was always brought there to spend her summers alone. It is filled, rather, by an obsessive anticipation of her mother's return. And among these memories, the moments the girl cherished most were the times of illness, when her mother would remain with her, no longer withholding the signs of her love:

> Mes plus douces impressions sont celles des années où elle revint aux Oublis, rappelée parce que j'étais malade . . . . [E]lle n'était plus alors que douceur et tendresse longuement épanchées sans dissimulation ni contrainte. (*JS*, p. 86)

Actual recovery, however, was undesirable, for it meant the departure of her mother, her principal standard of virtue, whose absence introduced a kind of moral isolation. Ideally convalescence would be extended indefinitely, placing the narrator always in a privileged position between illness and health, so that her mother's presence could be savored forever through the troubled anticipation of imminent departure. The period of suspension is emblematic of the narrative as a whole, for it preserves the girl's vision by placing the story of disillusionment between herself and the image of fullness. It postpones the discovery that the memories of untroubled innocence are already troubled by the loss of that innocence—and may even be the product of that loss.

In *La Place de la madeleine*, Serge Doubrovsky has pointed out an analogous strategy of recuperation through writing. By "psychoanalyzing" the text and the "fantasme" Marcel pursues, he is able to show the endlessness of the text, its "Penelope-like" quality:

> L'identification fantasmatique, qui a fait le texte, le défait. Une fois entré dans le système de l'Imaginaire, on n'en sort plus,—même par la mort. Tante Léonie a si bien installé sa vie réelle dans une mort imaginaire, que même sa vraie mort, quand elle survient, reste *fiction*. . . . [32]

For Doubrovsky, the search for a transparent language, for the convergence of reader and writer through the text, marks the illusory attempt to return to the mother:

> La fusion des images est un leurre, la pure identité de l'Alter et de l'Ego une chimère. . . . La lecture devient un piège à "prendre l'Autre," un stratagème pour retourner, une fois de plus, dans l'imaginaire, les rôles de domination réelle.[33]

Doubrovsky's study finds Marcel's project "fictif" because it is predicated on an impossible union with the other, whereas my analysis locates the impossibility of the project in the nature of the reading experience. We begin to perceive how the impossible desire mirrors, and therefore describes, that *textual* experience.

A la recherche du temps perdu is carefully built around the crucial conflict between the impossibility of literally grasping the fullness of a sign or experience and the complementary temptation to take Marcel and his text *à la lettre*. This is the struggle between the impossibility of seeing clearly and the irresistible urge to attempt just that. As the Vivonne passage indicates, the struggle is a continual one, one which constitutes and characterizes the narrative. The "illusions" Marcel entertains are never simply overcome, for his engagement with them paves the narrative path, that is, it forms the narrative. He does not suddenly become an artist at the novel's end, if only because his wandering is also the path to that objective. The movement of transformation is always occurring, like the conflict continually at work in John Ruskin between resistance to idolatry and acquiescence. The "duel" between these thrusts did not take place "à certaines heures de sa vie, non pas dans certaines pages de ses livres, mais à toute minute," and in the most profound, secret regions of the text (*CSB*, p. 130).

The theoretical passages of *Le Temps retrouvé*, rather than being disruptive or out of character for the work as some critics have found,[34] may be said to express a desire underlying the whole novel, albeit in contradiction to many of its insights. They reveal Marcel's—and quite possibly also Proust's—urge to escape from the conflict and complexity of the text and to speak out clearly. They would master the text and make direct statements whose efficacy the body of the narrative is denying. The novel arises from between these several directions and belongs to both "Marcel" and "Proust." Its special quality lies in the troubled nature of their difference and in the text's ability to form itself from these oppositions. *A la recherche* is the attempt to seize what it demonstrates cannot be seized; it interweaves the warning against the illusion of literality and the invitation to indulge that illusion. In the final chapters of this book, we will be examining the manipulation in the last part of the *Recherche* as Proust's implication in a strategy of recuperation. He will reveal his return to idolatry in his use of Marcel, but in a way which fulfills the lesson of the book; for the commission of the errors of idolatry and literality is a necessary part of the experience of the book—for Marcel, for Proust, and for the reader. The encounter with illusion is essential to performing the work, which is what the reader does. The reading must be a "sincere" encounter, for to avoid the error is to miss the point of the text. No perspective is fully outside this dialectic. From between each group of diverging tendencies in the novel there arises a new ground, capable of dynamically preserving the image of possibilities that is denied in more explicit form. This study begins by examining Proust in just such a reading encounter and follows the mystified projects of Marcel into the realms of desire and judgement. It ends by exploring the nature of Proust's vision, his own projects for his novel, and its potential for reconsecrating the fruits of idolatry.

1
The Pilgrimage: Proust Reads Ruskin

> *[J]e portais à mes lèvres une cuillerée du thé où j'avais laissé s'amollir un morceau de madeleine. Mais à l'instant même . . . [u]n plaisir délicieux m'avait envahi. . . .*
>
> —Marcel Proust
> *A la recherche du temps perdu*

John Ruskin represents an origin for Proust, yet also a turning point. He discovered the English critic while still in his twenties and for years was an avid disciple, writing numerous articles on him and translating two of his books. Upon Ruskin's death, in January 1900, he published four articles, revealing the reverence in which he held the man:

> Comprenant mal jusque-là la portée de l'art religieux au moyen âge, je m'étais dit, dans ma ferveur pour Ruskin: Il m'apprendra, car lui aussi, en quelques parcelles du moins, n'est-il pas la vérité? Il fera entrer mon esprit là où il n'avait pas accès, car il est la porte. Il me purifiera. (*CSB*, p. 104)[1]

Yet by the time he translates *Sesame and Lilies*, in 1905, Ruskin is merely a figure through which Proust establishes his own ideas about art. Jean Autret has noted the independence of opinion which is evident in "Sur la lecture," Proust's preface to his translation:

> Après avoir évoqué les souvenirs d'Illiers, et mettant hors de cause les lectures d'enfance dont il vient de signaler le pouvoir évocateur, Proust prend le contre-pied des idées de Ruskin. . . . Après avoir dénié à la lecture le rôle prépondérant que lui assigne Ruskin, Proust va signaler les limites du rôle de la lecture.[2]

What is most interesting about the limits of reading which Proust addresses is that they are being drawn with respect to his own reading of Ruskin. Between

1900 and 1905 there has occurred a radical change in his position toward his master, and the precise moment of this turnabout can be located in the preface to an earlier translation of Ruskin, *La Bible d'Amiens*. Proust's entire experience of Ruskin, which as it turns out has *always* been one of self-discovery, now reveals to him that all serious reading is a reading of one's self: "[L]a lecture n'agit qu'à la façon d'une incitation qui ne peut en rien se substituer à notre activité personnelle" (*CSB*, p. 180). But in the peculiar light of his own discovery of self, the encounter with Ruskin is expressed as a lesson in the dangers of reading:

> [Le rôle de la lecture] devient dangereux au contraire quand, au lieu de nous éveiller à la vie personnelle de l'esprit, la lecture tend à se substituer à elle, quand la vérité ne nous apparaît plus comme un idéal que nous ne pouvons réaliser que par le progrès intime de notre pensée et par l'effort de notre cœur, mais comme une chose matérielle, déposée entre les feuillets des livres comme un miel tout préparé par les autres et que nous n'avons qu'à prendre la peine d'atteindre sur les rayons des bibliothèques et de déguster ensuite passivement dans un parfait repos de corps et d'esprit. (*CSB*, pp. 180-81)

Reading offers the dangerous substitution of a "ready-made" idea, the adoption of another's clarity in the place of a true interiorization through adaptation of his text. Reading, Proust has learned through his encounter with Ruskin, tempts us to accept a quotation instead of forcing us to make an interpretation. The critical view he offers of Ruskin here stands in stark contrast to his earlier encomium. The question which must underlie any inquiry into Proust's own sense of his encounter with Ruskin is what causes him to persist in translating the Englishman's writings and commenting upon them at great length, even after the 1904 repudiation. The problem here is not to characterize Proust's interpretation of Ruskin nor the form in which that critic's aesthetic ideas appear in *A la recherche*; these questions have been ably dealt with elsewhere by others.[3] What remains to be explored here is rather the nature of the experience through which Proust turns away from his adulation of Ruskin: the textual moment when he confronts his own idolatrous reading and finds in the experience of idolatry one of the fundamental structures of his novel.

In his early articles, Proust assiduously follows his master's path to Amiens and to Venice, discovering the grandeurs of medieval art, as well as the workings of that exceptional mind. This period is a crucial one for Proust's aesthetic development, for the English critic reveals to him "le monde plus réel" in the art of these churches. Soon after writing these essays, Proust began work on a translation of Ruskin's *Bible of Amiens*, a careful and erudite guide to the cathedral of Notre-Dame d'Amiens. By the time the translation was completed in 1903, Proust's interest had cooled. For his preface he merely assembled the two long articles written in 1900, at the peak of his enthusiasm.

and appended a postscript most notable for its vehement criticism of the man he had once considered the "Prophet of Amiens":

> [I]l y a une sorte d'idolâtrie que personne n'a mieux définie que Ruskin. . . . Or, il semble bien qu'à la base de l'œuvre de Ruskin, à la racine de son talent, on trouve précisément cette idolâtrie. (*CSB*, p. 129)

Walter Strauss[4] suggests that Proust continued his translation, although his passion for Ruskin was past, to satisfy his mother's wishes and the memory of his late father, while George Painter[5] sees this repudiation as Proust's attempt to free himself from his subservient relationship to his master. But neither explanation resolves why Proust went on, after his 1904 repudiation, to translate Ruskin's *Sesame and Lillies* with extensive notes, nor why he included his early, extravagant essays in his preface to *La Bible d'Amiens* along with his repudiation. The answer must be sought in the preface itself, in its entirety, grasped as a self-conscious expression of an experience of reading.

The articles from 1900 show Proust articulating a broad sense of what the critic can and must accomplish, for Ruskin defines this role for him:

> Car l'homme de génie ne peut donner naissance à des œuvres qui ne mourront pas qu'en les créant à l'image non de l'être mortel qu'il est, mais de l'exemplaire d'humanité qu'il porte en lui. (*CSB*, p. 106)

There is a certain ambiguity introduced into these articles, to which we will return later. For Ruskin takes his reader on a pilgrimage to Amiens in order to open up the aesthetic and moral secrets of the cathedral, and Proust assumes the mission of performing this mediation for Ruskin's own secrets. He becomes an apostle for Ruskin the prophet, inviting his readers to follow Ruskin's path on a "pèlerinage ruskinien" to the places which "gardent son âme," on a voyage that is both a tribute to his master and an initiation to the church at Amiens. Yet Proust begins by carefully distinguishing his proposed pilgrimage from "[le] fétichisme qui n'est qu'illusion" (*CSB*, p. 70), the sort of fetichism that misleads lovers of Wagner by inspiring them to go to Bayreuth to hear his music. The town of Bayreuth, Proust implies, will add nothing to Wagner, but Ruskin's power as a creative critical mind can only be fully appreciated by visiting Notre-Dame d'Amiens. For his thought has a special quality which endears it to Proust: it goes out from itself, attaching itself to the particularity of the object it is observing, and assumes a physical dimension:

> Car la pensée de Ruskin n'est pas comme la pensée d'un Emerson par exemple, qui est contenue tout entière dans un livre, c'est-à-dire un quelque chose d'abstrait, un pur signe d'elle-même. L'objet auquel s'applique une pensée comme celle de Ruskin et dont elle est inséparable n'est pas immatériel, il est répandu çà et là sur la surface de la terre. Il faut aller le chercher là où il se trouve, à Pise, à Florence, à Venise. (*CSB*, p. 138)

Both Proust and Ruskin felt the need for a work of art to assume fully individual form, and both admired the great achievement of Gothic art in this respect. Proust sees Ruskin's attention to detail as the emblem of a forceful and imaginative critical faculty; details are the key to the success of the whole. In fact, Proust defends his master against the charge of "realism" by showing how details rarely remain simply themselves in Ruskin's interpretations. Although Ruskin is scrupulous in his accuracy, each detail grows in meaning in his perception until it becomes a metaphor for the whole work of art. In resurrecting the uniqueness of a tiny figure in the "Portail des Libraires" at Rouen, Proust sees Ruskin restoring to the universal work of art its essential particularity. The critic is the one who must bring the light of creative perception to old images, naming things by their names: "Voyez, c'est ceci, c'est cela" (*CSB*, p. 126). And his examples of metaphor, examined in detail, become lessons, for Proust, in the nature of metaphoric expression.

In his resistance to dealing with reality as "mere" detail, Ruskin, as the quintessential critic, is always engaged in locating "la réalité éternelle" and "fixer cette réalité" (*CSB*, p. 110). The job of every critic, in Proust's estimation, is to bring into relief the essential features of an artist's genius, and to accomplish this for Ruskin, he resorts to an unusual device which anticipates the structure of memory in *A la recherche*. On virtually each page of his translation, Proust develops, as a kind of continuous appendix to Ruskin's text, an extensive network of footnotes which complement the text with excerpts from other works by Ruskin. "Ne lire qu'un livre d'un auteur," Proust explains in a lengthy footnote, "c'est n'avoir avec cet auteur qu'une rencontre" (*CSB*, p. 75). Only through their repeated appearance in different contexts can the characteristics and essential traits of a writer be recognized:

> Nous retrouvons dans un second livre, dans un autre tableau, les particularités dont la première fois nous aurions pu croire qu'elles appartenaient au sujet traité. . . . En mettant une note au bas des passages de la *Bible d'Amiens* chaque fois que la texte éveillait par les analogies, même lointaines, le souvenir d'autres ouvrages de Ruskin . . . j'ai tâché de permettre au lecteur de se placer dans la situation de quelqu'un qui ne se trouverait pas en présence de Ruskin pour la première fois. (*CSB*, p. 75n)

With this artificial repertoire of previous encounters with Ruskin, this "improvised memory," the reader will now be able to recognize in Ruskin "ce qui est chez lui permanent et fondamental."[6] A critic must "reconstitute" what he perceives to be "la singulière vie spirituelle d'un écrivain," for this spiritual life is so haunted, for Proust, by the writer's special, personal realities that "talent" becomes the artist's ability to create this personal vision in his work. And the critic must ensure, in Proust's words, "une vision claire et durable" of these realities.

In the context of Proust's boundless enthusiasm, where Ruskin is clearly his exemplary critic, the violent attack and harsh tones of the postscript become even more startling. Yet Proust begins his repudiation in language that tries to assert its continuity with his former adoration. He cites the last lines of his 1900 article, insisting "Voici ce que je voulais dire," but now Ruskin is seen as having become caught in the mirage of his own words. Using the English critic's own definition, Proust finds that Ruskin has fallen prey to idolatry, the error of "servir avec le meilleur de nos cœurs et de nos esprits quelque chère ou triste image que nous nous sommes créée, pendant que nous désobéissons à l'appel présent du Maître" (*CSB*, p. 129). Suddenly, for Proust, the master's entire position has been undermined by a pervasive "insincerity":

> Or, il semble bien qu'à la base de l'œuvre de Ruskin, à la racine de son talent, on trouve précisément cette idolâtrie. Sans doute il ne l'a jamais laissée recouvrir complètement . . . et finalement tuer, sa sincérité intellectuelle et morale. A chaque ligne de ses œuvres comme à tous les moments de sa vie, on sent ce besoin de sincérité qui lutte contre l'idolâtrie, qui proclame sa vanité, qui humilie la beauté devant le devoir, fût-il inesthétique. (*CSB*, pp. 129-30)

"Idolatry" is the tendency to "[attacher] de l'importance excessive . . . à la lettre des œuvres" (*CSB*, p. 134), and in committing this sin Ruskin gets caught up in the aesthetics of his remarks, allowing the harmony of their expression to dictate their content. This forces him first to distort his thought and then to hide the actual grounds for his decision behind spurious "moral" reasons. Proust complains that Ruskin could not have been "entièrement sincère avec lui-même" when he found the crimes of the Venetians more inexcusable because they were committed in full view of St. Mark's, or as Proust put it, "parce que le palais des Doges était à côté de Saint-Marc au lieu d'être à l'autre bout de la ville" (*CSB* p. 132). Ruskin has been led, rather, to make an essentially moral judgement on unstated aesthetic grounds:

> Les doctrines qu'il professait étaient des doctrines morales et non des doctrines esthétiques, et pourtant il les choisissait pour leur beauté. Et comme il ne voulait pas les présenter comme belles, mais comme vraies, il était obligé de se mentir à lui-même. (*CSB*, p. 130)

Only a certain willfulness allows Ruskin to finish his chapter on Egypt by calling that land "l'éducatrice de Moïse et l'Hôtesse du Christ." Proust objects strongly that Ruskin's aesthetic self-indulgence, and not the content of his remarks, brought him to use certain expresssions, even to altering his thoughts in the interests of symmetry. The deliberate attempt to *impose* a harmony results, characteristically for Proust, in a beauty that rings false. There must result "un équilibre qui semble imposer à la pensée une ordonnance symétrique plutôt que le recevoir d'elle" (*CSB*, p. 134). For Ruskin is permitting the beauty of his thoughts, and of their expression, to conflict with their truthfulness, allowing the name "Egypt" to identify both the present "geographical" land and the biblical, historical concept. Yet somehow Proust's examples never quite convict Ruskin of the kind of idolatry he described in his initial definition.

The act of becoming caught in the "mirage des mots, des couleurs ou des belles formes" sounds far closer to the second kind of idolatry Proust discusses. Becoming so enamored of "quelque chère ou triste image que nous nous sommes créée" that we lose sight of the real nature of our object—this is the error of literality. This kind of idolater always notices that the outfit of a lady friend is "precisely" the dress from a specific novel or painting:

> [I]l reconnaît avec admiration dans l'étoffe où se drape une tragédienne, le propre tissu qu'on voit sur la Mort dans *Le Jeune homme et la Mort*, de Gustave Moreau, ou dans la toilette d'une de ses amies: "la robe et la coiffure mêmes que portait la princesse de Cadignan le jour où elle vit d'Arthez pour la première fois." (*CSB*, p. 135)

But this admiration, Proust points out, finds the dress beautiful only because it appears in a novel by Balzac and not by virtue of the intrinsic beauty of the dress nor because of the way it embodies Balzac's art; this fond admirer has become "touché par la noblesse de son souvenir":

> [I]l s'écrie: "C'est bien beau!" non parce que l'étoffe est belle, mais parce qu'elle est l'étoffe peinte par Moreau ou décrite par Balzac et qu'ainsi elle est à jamais sacrée . . . aux idolâtres. (*CSB*, p. 135)

The idolater locates the beauty of her dress outside the work of art, in an illusory similarity. Proust argues that the dress derives its beauty only from the work of art and from the role it played there; the friend's dress is simply irrelevant to Balzac's novel. On the basis of this false similarity, however, the idolater abstracts Balzac's creation from the framework of the novel and turns it into a real piece of clothing. Behind this operation is a deceptive literalism: the belief that we are dealing with the same dress. By ignoring the role the dress plays in the novel, the idolater mistakes the name for the object:

> La toilette de Mme de Cadignan est une ravissante invention de Balzac parce qu'elle donne une idée de l'art de Mme de Cadignan, qu'elle nous fait connaître l'impression que celle-ci veut produire sur d'Arthez. . . . Mais une fois dépouillée de l'esprit qui est en elle, elle n'est qu'un signe dépouillé de sa signification, c'est-à-dire, rien; et continuer à l'adorer, jusqu'à s'extasier de la retrouver dans la vie sur un corps de femme, c'est là proprement de l'idolâtrie. (*CSB*, p. 136)

In Proust's estimation, the "dress" is beautiful only because it expresses the project of Diane de Cadignan and the art of Balzac. The idolater strips it of its intentionality—yet through the "real" dress, in a inversion of priorities, he hopes to reach the secret of the beauty of Diane's dress.

The example is particularly well chosen because of the artfulness of the Princesse's project itself. The dress is important to Proust only because of the way it expresses the impression she wishes to produce. It articulates her skill at producing that impression and, especially, her ability to conceal that artfulness. Neither the "essence" of the dress's meaningfulness nor that of the text itself can be more closely approached or more truly possessed in the material dress than was already possible in the original reading of the novel. But idolatry is the indulgence of the illusion that such approach and possession are possible; it dissolves the crucial difference between the dress in a work of art and that seen in real life. Proust is attacking the notion that the work of art can be grasped at all through other means than direct confrontation. As he expressed it later in "La Méthode de Sainte-Beuve,"

> Il est trop facile de croire que [la vérité d'un œuvre d'art] nous arrivera un beau matin dans notre courrier, sous forme d'une lettre inédite qu'un bibliothécaire de nos amis nous communiquera. (*CSB*, p. 222)

But if his accusation of idolatry does not fit Ruskin, Proust is quite possibly making the charge against himself—especially as idolatry seems to describe his reading of Ruskin. Proust admits that he took Ruskin's guidance "à la lettre," even as he tried to free himself of the charge of excessive literality:

> Non, je ne trouverai pas un tableau plus beau parce que l'artiste aura peint au premier plan une aubépine, bien que je ne connaisse rien de plus beau que l'aubépine, car je veux rester sincère et que je sais que la beauté d'un tableau ne dépend pas des choses qui y sont représentées. (*CSB*, p. 137)

This error must be avoided, however, not simply as Proust claims here "because I wish to remain sincere," but because idolatry robs the work of art of, for Proust, its most cherished attribute: the ability to defy the reader's attempt to appropriate it. Proust's tone is one of excuse and self-justification, for even in his repudiation he reveals an alternation of sharp criticism and extravagant praise:

> C'est avec mes plus chères impressions esthétiques que j'ai voulu lutter ici, tâchant de pousser jusqu'à ses dernières et plus cruelles limites la sincérité intellectuelle. Ai-je besoin d'ajouter que, si je fais, en quelque sorte *dans l'absolu*, cette réserve générale moins sur les œuvres de Ruskin que sur l'essence de leur inspiration et la qualité de leur beauté, il n'en est pas moins pour moi un des plus grands écrivains de tous les temps et de tous les pays. (*CSB*, p. 134)

The relation to Ruskin revealed in the postscript is not simply a change from the earlier adoration, but contains that adoration in a state of uncertainty and flux. Ruskin's idolatry is troubling for Proust, finally, because the pilgrimage to which it invites him is not entirely unjustifiable. An idolatrous appreciation of Balzac's dress may have no real relationship to his novel—no more than Bayreuth does to the music of Wagner—but as Proust insisted even in his first essay, the journey to Amiens is in some way a necessary complement to Ruskin's text and quite different from a pilgrimage to his birthplace:

> Nous honorons d'un fétichisme qui n'est qu'illusion, une tombe où reste seulement de Ruskin ce qui n'était pas lui-même, et nous n'irions pas nous agenouiller devant ces pierres d'Amiens, à qui il venait demander sa pensée, et qui la gardent encore? (*CSB*, p. 70)

The power of Ruskin's imagination seems to find itself fully incarnated only in the cathedral, but because of this need to embody itself in a unique object, Ruskin's text always contains the potential for idolatrous literalism. The voyage to Bayreuth clearly cannot bring us closer to the mystery of Wagner, but visiting Amiens just may bring us closer to a grasp of Ruskin. The very term Proust selects describes someone who substitutes the cult of an idol for adoration of the true divinity, making the two synonymous—as though the spiritual could be possessed through its material manifestation. The danger for Proust is that the sanctity of the cathedral threatens to overflow into the text that talks about it. The union of word and place opens up the possibility that the secret of the text can be approached physically, much as Albertine, when she returns to Paris, seems to offer Marcel the elusive secret of Balbec:

> Il suffisait qu'on me dise qu'elle était à Paris et qu'elle était passée chez moi pour que je la revisse comme une rose au bord de la mer. Je ne sais trop si c'était le désir de Balbec ou d'elle qui s'emparait de moi alors, peut-être le désir d'elle étant lui-même une form paresseuse, lâche et incomplète de posséder Balbec, comme si posséder matériellement une chose . . . équivalait à la posséder spirituellement. (II, 351)

Proust followed Ruskin to Amiens because there seemed something special, even sacred, about the path his master had taken and the places he had visited. Unlike Bayreuth or Connestone, these were "véritables lieux de pèlerinage," where he hoped to "lire la Bible de Ruskin." Thus, quite mystified by the object of his quest, Proust embarked on a thoroughly idolatrous pilgrimage, eager to implement a formula for aesthetic truth. He traces Ruskin's path very much "à la lettre," happy to follow the "prescriptions ruskiniennes" (*CSB*, p. 82). And because they are mentioned in his "Bible" and may be the same ones Ruskin passed, even the beggars on the road to the cathedral are sanctified . . . for Proust. Since Ruskin is the source of truth, Proust will tread this path in faithful imitation because it must lead him back to that source:

[J]e m'étais dit, dans ma ferveur pour Ruskin: Il m'apprendra, car . . . n'est-il pas la vérité? Il fera entrer mon esprit là où il n'avait pas accès, car il est la porte. Il me purifiera, car son inspiration est comme le lys de la vallée. (*CSB*, p. 104)

The language, reminiscent of the Psalms, expresses a thoroughly religious attitude, but Proust's professed object is aesthetic: "la vision claire et durable" of the critic. By locating itself between the text (Ruskin's *Bible*) and the cathedral (Amiens' "Bible"), this religious language reveals Proust's fundamentally uncertain position. He has never been quite sure whether the object of his "pèlerinage ruskinienne" was the critic or the cathedral—Ruskin's text always lay between the poles of easy definition. "Not Amiens itself, but Amiens as it was re-created in the mind of Ruskin, was the object of his pilgrimage," remarks a perceptive critic.[7] His object is the image in the mind of Ruskin, but Proust's voyage was to the *real* cathedral.

In analogous fashion, Proust realized, a critic is caught between the particular and the general: he may neither focus on mere detail for its own sake, nor may he lose himself in abstractions. Indeed, the detail is important only in its relation to the whole, while abstractions are available only when they have already been particularized. The problem of successful mediation interested Proust greatly and caused him, in the conclusion to *Contre Sainte-Beuve*, to locate the essence of a painter "between" any two particular works: neither in the one nor the other, "mais . . . en quelque sorte . . . entre les deux, dans une sorte de tableau idéal" (*CSB*, p. 304). But whereas idolatry is the failure to make the distinction between literal and figurative elements, Ruskin's genius is often to exploit their interdependence. Proust emphasizes that the "eternal reality" of each church, for Ruskin, begins in its intimate relationship to "le charme de ces pays d'où elles surgirent." Ruskin himself is seen as an exemplary human being in the "présence d'une réalité éternelle," but his talent is his ability to "fix" that essence in a particularity. The position where Proust finds Ruskin's text—between detail and whole, between the particular and the eternal, between the book and the cathedral—thus makes that text a continual incitement to idolatry.

When Proust travels to Venice, it is to seize physically the secret of John Ruskin:

[J]e partis pour Venise afin d'avoir pu, avant de mourir, approcher, toucher, voir incarnées, en des palais défaillants mais encore debout et roses, les idées de Ruskin. (*CSB*, p. 139)

The attempt to surprise Ruskin's text through immediate contact affects every aspect of Proust's pilgrimage: the journey itself is rooted in the desire to transcend the text. And even when he appears most preoccupied with

The Pilgrimage

Ruskin's artistry, he betrays a compulsion to lead us to the exact spot where that artistry was accomplished. Ruskin seems constantly to be tempting Proust to the mystified movement from the text to the geographic place. The pilgrimage to Amiens is only a variation of an earlier trip to St. Mark's, made in order to grasp Ruskin's perceptions:

> Je me souviens de l'avoir lue [cette page] pour la première fois dans Saint-Marc même, pendant une heure d'orage et d'obscurité où les mosaïques ne brillaient plus que de leur propre et matérielle lumière et d'un or interne . . . ; l'émotion que j'éprouvais à lire cette page, parmi tous ces anges qui s'illuminaient des ténèbres environnantes, était très grande et n'était pourtant peut-être pas très pure. (*CSB*, p. 133)

In St. Mark's, Proust finds himself facing a sudden contradiction between truth and pleasure. Sincerity had once meant a harmony of beauty and truth, exemplified by the expression which receives its beauty purely from the justness of its content. It implied an openness that allowed the beauty to fulfill itself and assured a certain purity—until the field was invaded by idolatry. The sincerity was original: one *remained* sincere ("car je veux rester sincère") until this harmony was disturbed by the intrusion of idolatry. But Ruskin's text upsets this simple scheme, leading Proust into an unclear and mixed relationship: he is caught between a repudiation of his master's errors and the traces of adulation—in the troubled territory of "impure" pleasure. Most disturbing is the discovery that these passages where Ruskin's thought seems most to "turn egoistically toward itself," are in fact among his most beautiful. When he accuses Ruskin of idolatry, Proust admits, "je vais citer une de [ces pages] que je trouve les plus belles et où ce défaut est pourtant le plus flagrant" (*CSB*, p. 131). Proust travels to St. Mark's to read Ruskin, knowing full well the sin he is indulging in, and thus cannot help but be disturbed by the pleasure he feels. After denouncing the Englishman's lack of sincerity in his discussion of the sins of the Venetians, Proust confesses,

> Il n'en est pas moins vrai que ce passage des *Stones of Venice* est d'une grande beauté, bien qu'il soit assez difficile de se rendre compte des raisons de cette beauté. (*CSB*, p. 132)

Like the sinful pleasure he feels, this is a suspect beauty, for it seems to depend on something hollow and "wrong." He doesn't know what to make of it: "Et pourtant, il doit y avoir quelque vérité. Il n'y a pas à proprement parler de beauté tout à fait mensongère" (*CSB*, p. 132). In the postscript, Proust is trying to discover the reason for this troubling paradox, but he is at a loss to find the object which could legitimately evoke this pleasure. He cannot reconcile his enjoyment, that is, with its apparent source in falsity, nor is he willing to give up the conviction that beauty and truth are inseparable, "car le plaisir esthétique est précisément celui qui accompagne la découverte d'une vérité" (*CSB*, p. 132).

The pure harmony of original sincerity corresponds to a simpler moment in Proust's thought. His discovery of this paradoxical pleasure coincides with the realization that Ruskin has never been uncomplex. Just as the Englishman's text has always found its object between an idea and a religious edifice, his thought demonstrates *at every moment* the fundamental struggle between his "sincerity" and his "idolatry":

> [L]e véritable duel entre son idolâtrie et sa sincérité se jouait non pas à certaines heures de sa vie, non pas dans certaines pages de ses livres, mais à toute minute, dans ces régions profondes, secrètes, presque inconnues à nous-mêmes. (*CSB*, p. 130)

Idolatry can no longer be considered a separate outside force opposing and contaminating sincerity; the notion of this kind of simplicity is itself idolatrous. Rather, idolatry creates the difference between sincerity and insincerity and reveals the presence of both the "real" ("sincere") and the "artificial" ("insincere") in the mixed nature of pleasure and beauty. The text creates not only its "aura," the impossibility of its being possessed, but also, simultaneously, the illusory possibility of that possession. As Proust will later inscribe in his own great text, in the projects of possessing Balbec or Albertine, the text is both an incitement to idolatry and a lesson in the futility of the idolatrous project. The troubled pleasure Proust feels demonstrates that poetry finds its ground not in an uncomplex "sincerity," but in a middle ground between "sincerity" and "insincerity."

Proust placed his early essays side by side with his postscript because, in his exploration of the strange *trouble* he felt, he recognized the necessary link between idolatry and reading. His preface deliberately forms a history of his relationship to Ruskin and thus a lesson in idolatrous reading. If he prints both the early and later essays, it is because he senses that in the story of his encounter with Ruskin lies the structure of an "allegory" of error. Both the textual responses must be portrayed, the deception as well as the moment of recognition. This "story" lies at the heart of an entire aspect of Proust's work, as much of the following discussion will reveal. These same concerns are found in his later critical essays and in *Contre Sainte-Beuve*, but only with the complete *Recherche* does the structure of idolatry find its fullest expression. His experience of Ruskin lends a new sense of what "influence" implies, and only through understanding that experience can we begin to grasp the essentially *textual* nature of Marcel's numerous idolatrous projects. Only in this way can we glimpse *A la recherche du temps perdu* as an allegory of reading.

Our study began by trying to discover what lay behind the conflict in Proust's preface and what impelled him to reprint his adulatory essays despite his repudiation of Ruskin. Pure sincerity, he found, was never possible, and the pleasure he once felt in Ruskin turned out to have been grossly idolatrous. Yet even his repudiation expresses a longing for the simplicity he seems to have renounced, at times even retaining language which continues to imply the possibility of sincerity. The only pleasure remaining is perhaps troubled, but the text may still evoke the time when this was *not yet* the case. L. A. Bisson, in an excellent article,[8] introduces the possibility that Proust was impelled to his translation by an increasing nostalgia for his lost passion for Ruskin. And indeed we can see Proust recalling a simpler time in the past and a clearer, albeit idolatrous, relationship. His weakness indicates another paradigmatic quality of the text: the irresistibility of its illusion. At the end of his postscript, he reveals his intent with startling directness:

> Mais en parlant de cette passion . . . ne pouvant réveiller les flammes du passé, nous voulons du moins recueillir sa cendre. A défaut d'une résurrection dont nous n'avons plus le pouvoir, avec . . . la mémoire des faits qui nous dit: "tu étais tel" sans nous permettre de le redevenir, qui nous affirme la réalité d'un paradis perdu au lieu de nous le rendre dans le souvenir, nous voulons du moins le décrire et en constituer la science. (*CSB*, p. 141)

Ruskin is *recalled* even more vividly in Proust's memory perhaps than he was ever experienced. Critics thus often cite reminiscences from the postscript to depict Proust's enthusiasm, as does René de Chantal when he states, "Proust nous décrit dans sa préface à *la Bible d'Amiens* quels furent *alors* [italics added] ses sentiments."[9] In the *Recherche*, this project of recovery that we saw already in "La Confession d'une jeune fille" will assume many forms. It will be found in Marcel's attempt to capture, through travel to the real Balbec, the image he has embroidered for himself from the extravagant descriptions of Swann and Legrandin. It will permeate the urge to recapture in Albertine the passion he felt for the undifferentiated *jeune fille en fleurs* seen from a distance:

> Ce qui en avait fait, et non à cause d'Albertine, parallèlement à elle, quand j'étais seul, la douceur [de ces moments], c'était justement, à l'appel de moments identiques, la perpétuelle renaissance de moments anciens. (III, 478)

And much as Albertine will seem to offer Marcel that vision lost in the past, the recollection of Ruskin here appears to restore to Proust the image of a simpler time. But his attempt to recapture the lost passion for Ruskin fills him with *trouble*, the same disquiet he felt at the forbidden, impure pleasure in St. Mark's and which he will feel reading Nerval's *Sylvie*. This is the suspicion that the impossible—just for an instant perhaps—is still possible, which is why, even in 1906, when he writes to a friend of his feelings for Ruskin, the passion is past but not the "trouble délicieux":

> Et tout à l'heure, lisant un voyage de Ruskin, sentant mon cœur battre du désir de revoir les mêmes lieux, je me dis: "Si je ne l'aimais plus, m'embellirait-il encore l'univers, jusqu'à me consumer de désir et de regret en face d'un indicateur de chemin de fer?" Oui, mon amour pour Ruskin dure. Seulement quelquefois rien ne le refroidit comme de lire Ruskin.[10]

The mixed feeling remains, and for a moment Proust indulges the idolatrous possibility of going to the place of an idea, imagining to himself that he can board the train to Amiens and recover there his passion for Ruskin and the innocence of those years. By convicting his mentor of idolatry, Proust perhaps felt he was freeing himself from it. In *Sylvie*, however, he encounters a text which seems to encourage, and even demand, an idolatrous reading. Proust is beginning to realize how fiction operates *through* idolatry and how every text entices the reader into its irresistible illusion. In the effectiveness of "idolatry," Proust finds a powerful instrument for the construction of his own fiction. Eventually, he will incarnate this crucial disjunction into the "plaisir délicieux" of the madeleine, but he will first have to discover, through his reading of Nerval, how the illusion can be exploited.

2

The Magic Voyage: Proust Reads Nerval

*Le fou est la victime de la
rébellion des mots.*

—Edmond Jabès
(*Je bâtis ma demeure*)

In his brilliant essay on Proust, the German critic Walter Benjamin noted with appropriate understatement that "one does not always proclaim loudly the most important thing one has to say."[1] Proust's novel is not only characterized by its innumerable, quiet subtleties, but these hidden moments discover the nature of textuality in the contrast between explicit statement and silent undertone. Reading itself participates in this paradoxical structure, as Proust learns when he tries to recall the works which filled the hours of his childhood. He finds those days spent reading, which seemed not to have been lived at all because they were spent "idly" among his books, are those most vividly remembered:

> Il n'y a peut-être pas de jours de notre enfance que nous ayons si pleinement vécus que ceux que nous avons cru laisser sans les vivre, ceux que nous avons passés avec un livre préféré. (*CSB*, p. 160)

In this essay on reading, Proust encounters the play of absence and presence that reading creates. The lost days of his youth, which were filled with books rather than "experience," prove immune to the deterioration that attacks the past easily available to voluntary memory. Like involuntary memory, reading has preserved those days intact precisely because they seem never to have been lived in the first place. Reading can empty itself of its "own" content in order to encompass another. In attempting to talk about the readings of his childhood, Proust finds he has spoken of that childhood itself, of the memories he thought were irretrievably lost:

> [C]e que [les lectures] laissent surtout en nous, c'est l'image des lieux et des jours où nous les avons faites. Je n'ai pas échappé à leur sortilège: voulant parler d'elles,

j'ai parlé de toute autre chose que des livres parce que ce n'est pas d'eux qu'elles m'ont parlé. (*CSB*, p. 172)

Writing is also involved in this movement, for as Benjamin remarked, Proust "turned his days into nights"[2] as the "nocturnal" experience of writing came to replace totally the "real" daylight moments of which fiction was once presumed to be a reflection or recollection. Writing became more than the preservation of past experience; it became that experience itself.

One of the most important figures hidden in the labyrinthine structure of the *Recherche* stands very quietly there, and even though Proust, in his article on Flaubert, praised Gérard de Nerval as "un des trois ou quatre plus grands écrivains du XIXe siècle" (*CSB*, p. 596), his importance for Proust's novel has hardly been fully appreciated. His name is mentioned only twice in the *Recherche*, but his presence is profound, and in Marcel's drama of sleeping and waking, there is an unmistakable echo of the dilemma faced earlier by the narrator of *Sylvie*. Studies of their relationship have tended to examine Nerval's "influence" on Proust, reducing often to a description of their "common concerns."[3] The most fruitful confrontation between them occurs not in the *Recherche*, however, but in the fragments found in *Contre Sainte-Beuve*. Written around 1908, while Proust was still preoccupied with his search for a form for his novel, the essay "Gérard de Nerval" redefines *Sylvie*, revealing the crucial role of reading in Proust's project, and offers Proust insights into the nature of fiction which bring him closer to his own finished novel.

Although *Contre Sainte-Beuve* is incomplete in form and uncertain in objective, it is as much Proust's exploration of his own conception of literature and criticism as a frontal attack on the foremost French critic of the nineteenth century.[4] His editor tells us, "Proust ne songe à attaquer Sainte-Beuve que pour exposer par ce biais ses propres idées sur l'art et sur la critique,"[5] but this neglects Proust's real concern for the detrimental effect of Sainte-Beuve's method of criticism. His objective is to demonstrate Sainte-Beuve's error, refute his method, and reexamine the nature of fiction and reading:

Il me semble que j'aurais ainsi à dire sur Sainte-Beuve . . . qu'en montrant en quoi il a péché, à mon avis, comme écrivain et comme critique, j'arriverais peut-être à dire, sur ce que doit être la critique et ce qu'est l'art, quelques choses auxquelles j'ai souvent pensé. (*CSB*, p. 219)

Already in the essays on Ruskin, as we have seen, Proust was criticizing erroneous modes of reading, stressing that reading must elicit an active exploration "au fond de nous-mêmes," and warning against the temptation to look outside our own critical act for a truth hidden away in some purely external place. Proust found such maneuvers aimed at avoiding confrontation which the work of literature demands, and his admonitions anticipate the narrator's insistence, in the *Recherche*, that the text must be individually decoded: "Ce que nous n'avons pas eu à déchiffrer, à éclaircir par notre effort personnel, ce qui était clair avant nous, n'est pas à nous" (III, 880). He saw the concern with external artifacts as a false relief from the real problems of interpretation:

> [L]a vérité ne nous apparaît plus comme un idéal que nous ne pouvons réaliser que par le progrès intime de notre pensée et par l'effort de notre cœur, mais comme une chose matérielle, déposée entre les feuillets des livres comme un miel tout préparé par les autres. . . . [Parfois] la vérité, conçue comme extérieure encore, est lointaine, cachée dans un lieu d'accès difficile. (*CSB*, pp. 180-81)

These indictments of misreading culminate in Proust's famous attack on Sainte-Beuve's biographical method:

> La fameuse méthode . . . consiste à ne pas séparer l'homme et l'œuvre. . . . [C]ette méthode méconnaît ce qu'une fréquentation un peu profonde avec nous-même nous apprend: qu'un livre est le produit d'un autre moi que celui que nous manifestons dans nos habitudes, dans la société, dans nos vices. (*CSB*, pp. 221-22)

It hardly seems just to hypothesize a "naive materialism" for Sainte-Beuve, as Richard Terdiman does, and then accuse Proust of failing to appreciate "Sainte-Beuve's attempt to base explanation of a writer's work on the material circumstances in which it was produced."[6] While Proust does "define art and its criticism as autonomous realms of mental activity,"[7] his attack on Sainte-Beuve is clearly aimed at the deficiency of that critic's readings. It is not as though Sainte-Beuve were the misunderstood social critic of the nineteenth century; for Proust, he has hopelessly distorted the major writers of his time precisely by not reading their works and by supplementing that inadequacy through recourse to their social presence, their friends, and their conversations.

In Proust's mind, Sainte-Beuve sinned against the text by refusing to recognize the special nature of the authorial voice. And his willingness to exchange the work of art for the artist's conversation compromises the *difference* of fictional language. Sainte-Beuve has presumed that the social voice of an author is identical to the artistic, just as the visitor to Venice—or Illiers—imagines he is closer to the center of the works of Ruskin or of Proust. His method effaces the crucial distinction between the novelist seen in public and heard in his most private voice in his art. In a preparatory sketch for his novel, Proust created Mme de Villeparsis, a parody of Sainte-Beuve, who offers her friends a privileged impression of Balzac:

> "Je l'ai vu une fois chez [Mme de Castries], quand j'étais toute jeune mariée, c'était un homme très commun, qui n'a dit que des choses insignifiantes, et je n'ai pas voulu qu'on me le présente."[8]

This method cultivates a serious error, for it reinforces the illusion that external details, facts, and conversation will bring the critic closer to the heart of a work. But conversation is dangerously deceptive; Proust warns, "En réalité, ce qu'on donne au public, c'est ce qu'on a écrit seul, pour soi-même." Conversation has only the *appearance* of interiority:

> Ce n'est que l'apparence menteuse de l'image qui donne ici quelque chose de plus extérieur et de plus vague. . . . Ce qu'on donne à l'intimité, c'est-à-dire à la conversation (si raffinée soit-elle, et la plus raffinée est la pire de toutes, car elle fausse la vie spirituelle en se l'associant . . .) c'est l'œuvre d'un soi bien plus extérieur. (*CSB*, p. 224)

Following the dictates of his method, Proust finds, Sainte-Beuve misjudged the worth of Flaubert and Balzac, maligned the work of Stendhal, and failed to understand Baudelaire. But Gérard de Nerval was simply dismissed out of hand. Referring to a quotation from the great critic on the subject, "Gérard de Nerval était comme le commis voyageur littéraire de Paris à Munich," Proust responds with surprise, "Ce jugement semble surprenant aujourd'hui où on s'accorde à proclamer *Sylvie* un chef d'œuvre" (*CSB*, p. 233). Yet Proust is concerned by how misguidedly his contemporaries have admired *Sylvie*, seeing it only as an idealized portrait of prerevolutionary France. They seem to share a decidedly decorous, *convenable* reading of the story and the kind assurance that Nerval was a man clearly limited by history and place to a kind of local color and charm:

> Il est convenu aujourd'hui que Gérard de Nerval était un écrivain du XVIIIe siècle attardé et que le romantisme n'influença pas, un pur Gaulois, traditionnel et local, qui a donné dans *Sylvie* une peinture naïve et fine de la vie française idéalisée. (*CSB*, p. 233)

Proust reacts exasperatedly, however, in a manner strangely reminiscent of Sainte-Beuve:

> Voilà ce qu'on a fait de cet homme qui à vingt ans traduisait *Faust*, allait voir Goethe à Weimar, pourvoyait le romantisme de toute son inspiration étrangère . . . (*CSB*, p. 233)

He appears to be arguing that a man of such violent emotions, attracted to so powerful and Germanic a work as *Faust*, would not be likely to invest his mature energies in a pastoralized vision of "la vieille France." This was a man, he continues, whose extreme subjectivity and nostalgia led him to madness and, ultimately, to his mysterious death:

> [Cet homme qui] était dès sa jeunesse sujet à des accès de folie, était finalement enfermé, avait la nostalgie de l'Orient et finissait par y partir, était trouvé pendu à la poterne d'une cour immonde. . . . (*CSB*, pp. 233-34)

Proust seems to be asking how the work of a man may be dismissed as "traditionnel, bien Français," whose energies and inner turmoil led him to a deranged life and a stranger death. His apparently "biographical" argument sounds odd, however, in light of his criticism of Sainte-Beuve, for it seems to presuppose a continuity between the man Nerval and the author. The contradiction must be resolved through Proust's insight that Nerval's peculiarly subjective perception of the world is both thematically and structurally at the heart of *Sylvie*.

In a manner now characteristic for Proust, especially in *Contre Sainte-Beuve*, the subject is introduced by way of a misreading. He claims that he would even prefer the oblivion in which Sainte-Beuve left Nerval to the esteem which *Sylvie* now enjoyed, based on all the wrong reasons:

> Le dirai-je pourtant, *Sylvie* est admirée aujourd'hui si à contresens à mon avis, que je préférerais presque pour elle l'oubli où l'a laissée Sainte-Beuve et d'où du moins elle pouvait sortir intacte, dans sa miraculeuse fraîcheur. (*CSB*, p. 233).

Proust's essay is first of all a correction: contemporaries have read *Sylvie* literally, accepting the narrator Gérard's dream of the Valois as an objectively realistic picture. Proust singles out Jules Lemaitre, who in his book on Racine, found *Sylvie* a perfect description of the idyllic landscape where Racine may have spent his childhood:

> L'histoire se passe dans le pays même de Racine, le Valois. Elle sent à chaque page la vieille France . . . : "Des jeunes filles dansaient en rond sur la pelouse . . . "[9]

"Rien n'est plus loin de *Sylvie!*" Proust replies. "Il faut remettre cette phrase où elle est, dans son éclairage. C'est dans une sorte de rêve" (*CSB*, p. 235). This reading of *Sylvie* grows out of an excessive literalism, willing to accept Nerval's descriptions *à la lettre* as realistic descriptions of the French countryside. But Proust wants to differentiate Nerval's intentional use of narrative description and restore the complexity behind the apparent simplicity of *Sylvie*: "Cette histoire que vous appelez une peinture naïve, c'est le rêve d'un rêve" (*CSB*, p. 237). These scenes have only the appearance of simplicity and reality and depict the narrator's image of a place he thinks he remembers, a reality invaded by dreams: "Donc ce que nous avons ici, c'est un de ces tableaux d'une couleur irréelle, que nous n'avons pas dans la réalité" (*CSB*, p. 235). These tableaux create a disturbing *fraîcheur* in the same way as the image of the bottles lying in the Vivonne, and they remind us less of the countryside, Proust adds, than of other literary moments:

> Vous avez reconnu immédiatement cette poésie de Gérard:
>
> *Il est un air pour qui je donnerais . . .* (*CSB*, p. 235)

Such descriptions and scenes must not be separated from their origin in the story, for they express the narrator's predicament, his inability to locate the Loisy of his dreams or to orient himself in the world of reality.

Proust has perceived that for Nerval reality is itself never a simple matter, and he discovers here the continuity between Nerval's "madness" and his art. His reinterpretation, and the liberation of Nerval from the mask of simplicity, follow Proust's central insight that Nerval's *folie* was a radical extension of the "subjectivisme excessif" which characterizes the world of his stories. The innocence of this landscape, Proust insists, like the innocence of his language, is illusory. The narrative arises from a mind haunted by insomnia, madness, nostalgia and regret. "Reality" is always already tinged with the unreal and corrupted by dream and desire. The simple readings of *Sylvie* mistake the narrator's vision of the Valois for a realistic description and overlook the intricately subjective nature of the work. The landscape itself, Proust cautions, is recollected through memory and dream, even while Gérard is returning there in the middle of the night. And beyond the blur of insomnia, these memories are deeply marked by Gérard's hope of recovering the innocence he knew there. The whole is built on several layers of complication which at times lose the reader, just as they dislocate and confound the narrator:

> Et en évoquant ce temps dans un tableau de rêve, [Gérard] est pris du désir de partir pour ce pays . . . [il] prend une voiture, et tout en allant en cahotant vers Loisy, il se rappelle et raconte. Il arrive après cette nuit d'insomnie, et ce qu'il voit alors, pour ainsi dire détaché de la réalité par cette nuit d'insomnie, par ce retour . . . est entremêlé si étroitement aux souvenirs qu'il continue à évoquer, qu'on est obligé *à tout moment* [italics added] de tourner les pages qui précèdent pour voir où on se trouve, si c'est présent ou rappel du passé. (*CSB*, pp. 237-38)

The place to which Gérard is returning is already fictional. Proust recognizes the narrative as a disjunction of realities which makes *Sylvie* a disturbing work in the guise of a pastoral idyl. If he mentions Nerval's madness, it is to pierce the innocent surface of his fiction. He refuses to separate Nerval's *folie* from the rest of his life and isolate it into an aberration of his "rational" self:

> Fou, non pas d'une folie en quelque sorte purement organique et n'influant en rien sur la nature de la pensée, comme nous en avons connu de ces fous qui en dehors de leurs crises avaient plutôt trop de bon sens. . . . (*CSB*, p. 234)

Proust insists that this *folie* is rather a continuation, an exaggeration perhaps, of Nerval's style, of his very personal way of seeing the world. And like Ruskin's struggle against idolatry, Nerval's complex vision—madness *and* art—is present in every aspect of his perception:

> Chez Gérard de Nerval la folie naissante et pas encore déclarée n'est qu'une sorte de subjectivisme excessif, d'importance plus grande pour ainsi dire, attachée à un

rêve, à un souvenir, à la qualité personnelle de la sensation, qu'à ce que cette sensation signifie de commun à tous, de perceptible pour tous, la réalité. (*CSB*, p. 234)

The complexity of Nerval's "mad" vision was translated into the irreducible intricacy of his art:

> Et quand cette disposition qui est au fond la disposition artistique . . . finit par devenir la folie, cette folie est tellement le développement de son originalité littéraire dans ce qu'elle a d'essentiel, qu'il la décrit au fur et à mesure qu'il l'éprouve. (*CSB*, p. 234)

Above all, perhaps, Proust appreciated Nerval's mastery at depicting the dream's usurpation of reality. The countryside has become less a geographic fact here than an expression of Gérard's desire, "un pays qui est plutôt pour lui un passé qui existe au moins autant dans son cœur que sur la carte" (*CSB*, p. 238). Every moment of *Sylvie* must be read as participating in that "autant," as much in Gérard's fantasy as in the reality "commun à tous." The story is formed by the interweaving of these strands of dream and reality, and by Gérard's struggle to determine *where* he is. He narrates, as Proust indicates, while he is trying to return to a world of simplicity he thinks he remembers, hoping to recover an ideal already complex, "le souvenir d'une femme qu'il aimait en même temps qu'une autre" (*CSB*, p. 237). But the moment that recovery seems truly possible, Gérard becomes totally disoriented, unable to distinguish past from present, memory from history. The "Nerval" of Proust's discussion is thus no simple figure from "real life," from whose conversations and conduct the novel will be judged; he expresses rather, in his "madness," the complexity of the entire narrative. The similarity to Sainte-Beuve is ironic, for this *folie* is a *textual* madness. Nerval portrays his movement into this madness "comme un artiste noterait en s'endormant les états de conscience qui conduisent de la veille au sommeil, jusqu'au moment où le sommeil rend le dédoublement impossible" (*CSB*, p. 234). The point at which this *dédoublement* becomes impossible signals Gérard's entrance into the labyrinth of fiction: orientation is no longer possible.

Proust senses that the calm surface of Nerval's text is everywhere troubled by the narrator's tortured effort to situate himself, "se définir laborieusement à lui-même" (*CSB*, p. 237). As Proust wrote in an essay on Ruskin, the critic's task is to distinguish the significant aspects of a work, "les nommant de leur nom, il dit: 'Voyez, c'est ceci, c'est cela' " (*CSB*, p. 126). He must distinguish the charming surface of *Sylvie* from its source in Gérard's uneasy desire. This is a troubled and troubling work, drawn in violent colors, "en velours pourpre ou violacée, et nullement les tons aquarellés de leur France modérée" (*CSB*, p. 239). And Proust reacts violently to the misreading of Gérard's vision as charming and traditional. For Gérard is also a reader here, desperately attempting to make sense of the world he perceives and to distinguish dream from reality. For Proust, *Sylvie* is the story of the madness that structures the narrative and of Gérard's attempt to master his "excessive subjectivity" and escape the maddening complexity of the text.

Gérard returns, hoping to find at Valois the clarity and innocence he recalls. Life there existed in an unambiguous present: place names referred not to a vague memory, but to a distinct place and to the rural simplicity to which he could return every year. That was a time when orientation was still possible. But the Valois has become a labyrinthine fiction of past and present, memory and desire, into which Gérard falls, succumbing to the nature of his own language: reality and dream seem to converge at the proper name. Proust recognizes the idolatrous attempt to identify a figurative, literary reality with its real counterpart. Gérard imagines that the world of his childhood—*as he remembers* it—will be found where he left it and that he can reach this memory by identifying it as a real locale. In a similar attempt, Marcel will travel to Balbec, or embrace Albertine, hoping to find there the cathedral, or the woman, of his imagination. This "geographic" mystification, a deliberate confusion of realities, enacted through the name which the two "places" share, is clearly improper and a perversion of the critical act of naming. All the more interesting, then, is Proust's revalorization of Nerval's idolatry.

Reading *Sylvie*, Proust senses the chilling "fraîcheur" which marks with "inquiétude" the dislocation of simple reality. These tableaux are neither built along the lines of Lemaitre's "claires architectures" nor drawn in "claires et faciles aquarelles." Yet these scenes succeed in creating a superbly believable image of the Valois. The failure of the simple, realistic readings is a tribute to the force of the illusion Nerval has created. The great achievement of his fiction, for Proust, lies in the irresistible verisimilitude of his landscape: "Certes le tableau présenté par Gérard est délicieusement simple. Et c'est la fortune unique de son génie" (*CSB*, p. 239). Illusion is only effective when it can remain invisible, generating an appearance sufficiently seamless to hide the traces of art. There is a certain success, which Proust doubtless enjoys, in Nerval's ability to fool his reader with a surface whose flawlessness reminds him perhaps of "le poli de la surface" toward which Flaubert strove.[10] The success of the illusion makes possible the "sincère"[11] attempt to reach the lost vision in the real world. Within the terms of this attempt, Proust invokes the notion of *sincérité*, the desirer's commitment to the possibility of reaching the desired object, and of *trouble*, the sense of the gap between the incommensurable planes of fictional and empirical reality. Through them, Proust expresses the metaphor of Gérard's geographical mystification and the structure for Marcel's many attempts to cross the distance of desire.

Gérard's image of the Valois is so vivid that it hides the desire which is its source, and the possibility of his return is so real that the countryside he recalls becomes indistinguishable from the geographical site. The commitment to his illusion, the "sincerity" of his project, is proven by his journey to the actual place, Loisy:

> Mais Gérard allait revoir le Valois pour composer *Sylvie*? Mais oui. La passion croit son objet réel, l'amant de rêve d'un pays veut le voir. Sans cela, ce ne sera pas sincère. (*CSB*, pp. 241-42)

Sincérité describes the grounds for Gérard's attempt, the acceptance of the real possibility of recovering an illusion in the real world, of reaching geographically the country—or the woman—that exists only in the imagination. A recurrent image of this temptation in Proust is the railroad train: he feels the delicious *trouble* of possibility when the names called out suggest, without leaving the train, that he has entered a fictional landscape. *Sincérité* is the opening up of the possibility of seeing clearly, of finding a direction clear enough to establish a firm orientation. Gérard is so lost that he believes the return to Sylvie, who is the image of his lost innocence, will restore that innocence. This is a mystification that distinguishes Nerval from more sophisticated writers, but which gives his work its force. The more worldly writers, who save themselves the trouble of the useless voyage, can never produce a *Sylvie*, for the highly self-conscious writer has surrendered certain possibilities:

> On ne peut pas avoir fait avec l'intelligence et le goût un paysage, même comme Victor Hugo . . . et avoir empreint un pays de cette atmosphère de rêve que Gérard a laissée en Valois, parce que c'est bien de son rêve qu'il l'a tirée. (*CSB*, p. 241)

"Gérard est naïf et voyage," following his dream to its apparent source, while "Marcel Prévost se dit: restons chez nous, c'est un rêve" (*CSB*, p. 242).

Nerval's text is able to duplicate Gérard's mystification; these scenes charm the reader by placing him *between* fiction and reality, making him participate in the desire and confusion of the narrative. When Proust hears the names "Pontarmé" or "Chantilly" from a train, he also imagines he is traveling through the countryside of *Sylvie*. But Gérard's landscape is the opposite of realism, expressing the absence of the scene it describes, and it affects us as no real landscape could. Praises of real places "nous laissent froids," Proust remarks, but Nerval has impregnated these names from *Sylvie*, so that they "exaltent jusqu'à l'ivresse la pensée que nous pouvons par un beau matin d'hiver, partir, aller voir les pays, ces pays de rêve, où se promena Gérard" (*CSB*, p. 241). The narrative draws the reader into Gérard's mystification, which is itself essentially an error of reading. As he will do later in the *Recherche*, Proust draws attention to the experience of the proper name, the point at which the worlds of fantasy and reality appear to converge. The name seems to present the possibility of reaching one world through the other, offering the assurance of identity. Within the name, the geographical entity

Loisy is no different from the site of Gérard's remembered childhood innocence. It succeeds in hiding, for a moment, the crucial difference between realities. Proust is able to overcome this illusion almost immediately, but only at the cost of knowing the terrible gap between the worlds joined at their name. These landscapes charm us, but our pleasure is troubled:

> Certes, nous nous rappelons l'ivresse de ces premières matinées d'hiver, le désir du voyage ... mais notre plaisir est fait de trouble. (*CSB*, p. 240)

In this "trouble délicieux," Proust seems to find again the "impure joy" he felt years earlier reading Ruskin in the darkness of St. Mark's, but instead of condemning Nerval's idolatry, he praises his provocative genius:

> Certes, le tableau présenté par Gérard est délicieusement simple. Et c'est la fortune unique de son génie. Ces sensations si subjectives, si nous disons seulement la chose qui les provoque, nous ne rendons pas précisément ce qui leur donne du prix à nos yeux. Mais aussi, si nous essayons en analysant notre impression de rendre ce qu'elle a de subjectif, nous faisons évanouir l'image et le tableau. De sorte que par désespoir nous alimentons encore mieux nos rêveries avec ce qui nomme notre rêve sans l'expliquer, avec les indicateurs de chemin de fer, les récits de voyageurs.... (*CSB*, p. 239)

Nerval succeeds in evoking a middle ground *between* imagination and reality: his narrative is disturbing because it confronts the reader with a sensation to which *no* simple object—real *or* imagined—corresponds. His position is like that of Proust struggling to come to terms with Ruskin's idolatry. Finding his mentor's idolatrous pages inexplicably among his most beautiful, Proust is at a loss to locate the object which could legitimately evoke that beauty, "car le plaisir esthétique est précisément celui qui accompagne la découverte d'une vérité" (*CSB*, p. 132).

Already then Proust glimpsed a solution: "Et peut-être cette page des *Stones of Venice* était-elle belle surtout de me donner précisément ces joies mêlées que j'éprouvais dans Saint-Marc" (*CSB*, p. 133). Though Gérard cannot preserve his Valois in the name, yet these tableaux, like the days spent reading, carve a fictional time out of everyday life, magically preserving their context:

> Telles sont ces matinées bénies, creusées ... dans la dure pierre de nos journées, et gardant miraculeusement les couleurs délicieuses ... dans notre souvenir comme une grotte merveilleuse, magique et multicolore dans son atmosphère spéciale. (*CSB*, p. 239)

Nerval's special success is literary: he has been able to endow real places with the aura—and the depth—of poetry. This "unreal color" Proust finds, and which he first noticed while seeking Ruskin in Venice, is itself a literary dimension, woven into the scene by the narrative presence of the past:

> *La Divine comédie*, les pièces de Shakespeare, donnent aussi l'impression de contempler, inséré dans l'heure actuelle, un peu de passé; cette impression si exaltante qui fait ressembler certaines "Journées de lecture" à des journées de flânerie à Venise, sur la Piazetta [sic] par exemple, quand on a devant soi, dans leur couleur à demi irréelle de choses situées à quelques pas et à bien des siècles. . . . (*CSB*, p. 194)

The misreaders of *Sylvie* have missed this depth because their perception goes no further than the attractive surface of Nerval's narrative. Having accepted as a geographical reality the landscape which Gérard only imagines and desires, they commit, in a sense, the "wrong" error: closing up the text by embracing its literal elements. When Proust's ideal reader seizes upon "ce qui nomme notre rêve," he nevertheless knows the futility of his effort. The troubling sensation marks his awareness of the separation which should exist between the figural world and geographical reality. The Jules Lemaitres surely distort *Sylvie*, but without a clearer sense of Proust's main concerns while reading Nerval, it is difficult to understand the intensity of his reaction.

There is an undertone of impatience in Proust's essay to be heard, for instance, in his insistence that *Sylvie* partakes *in no way* ("nullement") of an atmosphere of moderation. "Rien n'est plus loin de *Sylvie!*" (*CSB*, p. 237) was his annoyed response to suggestions of amiability and charm. "Que cela est à cent lieues de Gérard!" (*CSB*, p. 240). His exasperation with these easy readers, and with their comfortable satisfaction, surely reflects his own frustrated attempts at the literary success he admires in Nerval. He vents his feelings by pointing out the inadequacies of the greatest writers; even Hugo cannot match Nerval:

> On peut penser sans trouble à l'admirable *Villequier* d'Hugo, à l'admirable *Loire* de Heredia. On frissonne quand on a lu dans un indicateur de chemin de fer le nom de Pontarmé. Il y a en lui quelque chose d'indéfinissable, qui se communique, qu'on voudrait par calcul avoir brut, mais qui est un élément original, qui entre dans la composition de ces génies et n'existe pas dans la composition des autres . . . comme il y a dans le fait d'être amoureux quelque chose de plus que dans l'admiration esthétique et de goût. (*CSB*, p. 241)

Nerval's story, for Proust, transgresses the boundaries between the real and the imaginary by creating a language that opens up the *jeu* between these realms and makes the reader an accomplice to this impropriety. Proust is infuriated that this delicate web of complexity, which is so troubling for him, can be read as a tableau of simplicity, that this story of transgression and guilt is received as the embodiment of innocence. His anger is expressed in his choice of an image to indict this reading:

> [C]'est comme si l'on trouvait qu'une classe de choses absolument pareilles sont un verre d'eau fraîche et un fiévreux, parce qu'il le désire, ou l'innocence d'une jeune fille et la lubricité d'un vieillard parce que la première est le rêve du second. (*CSB*, p. 236)

The calmness of Proust's essay is shocked by the violence of his comparison and by the implication that Gérard himself is the lubricious old man. Proust is insisting, thereby, that Gérard's earliest memories are in fact far from untroubled. They reveal not an atmosphere of innocence and simplicity, but the desire for that simplicity. They express the violent disorientation that leads Gérard to believe that the difference between the Loisy of his imagination and the actual town can be overcome by their common name, that he can find one woman in the person of another, "Cette Adrienne qu'il croit être la comédienne . . . et qui n'était pas elle" (*CSB*, p. 238). The innocence Gérard is seeking is the pure langauge which would allow several women to embody one ideal Woman, but even the Sylvie he finds is invariably "différente d'elle-même" each time he revisits her. For Proust, *Sylvie* is everywhere complex and troubled, its story growing out of "le souvenir d'une femme que [Gérard] aimait en même temps qu'une autre" (*CSB*, p. 237). The entire narrative participates in this complexity, and the innocent dance Lemaitre is recalling is actually a ceremony marking Gérard's transgression and his first infidelity: the destruction of his childhood idyl by the entrance of Adrienne.

In presenting Gérard as a lubricious old man chasing the figure of a young girl, Proust is reinforcing the violent context of *Sylvie*, and restoring the complexity of Gérard's desire. If these mornings are "real," they nevertheless evoke a disquieting exaltation: "La couleur juste de chaque chose vous émeut comme une harmonie, on a envie de pleurer de voir que les roses sont roses" (*CSB*, p. 238). This is not a moderate tale, vindicating the search for innocence; *Sylvie* is part of the fiery *Filles du feu*, the troubling story of innocence irretrievably lost—if ever it existed. When Proust notices this rose color in *Sylvie*, it is anything but the blush of a young girl's cheek:

> La couleur de *Sylvie*, c'est une couleur pourpre, d'une rose pourpre en velours pourpre ou violacée. . . . A tout moment ce rappel de rouge revient, tirs, foulards rouges, etc. Et ce nom lui-même pourpré de ses deux *i*: Sylvie, la vraie Fille du Feu. (*CSB*, p. 239)

Proust's reading works to strip away the deceptive raiments of the text, to penetrate its seemingly innocent surface. His image of brutal desire reintroduces the forgotten violence into the story, justifying the reader's need to get at the text and to go beneath its charming appearance. The relation between literal and figurative elements of language, as Gérard's projects have shown, is one of violence, transgressing each other's *property*. Through Proust's image, the act of reading is itself revealed as a violation with the reader in the role of the *vieillard*. Yet perhaps we should not be so surprised by this sudden turn in Proust's style, for he has already introduced the possibility of such a "strong" reading in his opening remarks, where he proposed to rescue *Sylvie*'s purity from the corruption of misreadings. Recall that Proust preferred the "oubli" in which Sainte-Beuve's opinion left *Sylvie* and from which "du moins elle pouvait sortir intacte" (*CSB*, p. 233). The integrity of the text, he is suggesting, will be better preserved in the claustration offered by Sainte-Beuve's neglect than by the readings which profess not to touch the text, reading it *à la lettre*. The "elle" who emerges is purposely ambiguous, evoking at once the girl and the story of the same name. The assurance that "she" is admired invites sexual connotations which are corroborated by Proust's hope that she will emerge "intact" from Sainte-Beuve's protective *oubli*, her freshness unsullied.

Nerval has made language apply enticingly to several worlds, and now Proust has joined in with a play on the referentiality of the name "Sylvie." Proust's critical project thus becomes analogous to Gérard's: protecting *Sylvie*'s purity from the perversion of distortion. The possibility of preservation implies an original textual integrity in the same way as Gérard's quest asserts the possibility of return to his childhood innocence. Yet this is more than just Proust's play on words: Nerval has corrupted the simplicity of ordinary language by making it refer to his own dream. Proust perceives that by interweaving names so that they refer indistinguishably to real and imaginary worlds, Nerval's text has been able to engage the reader in the narrator's mystified project of recovery. *Sylvie* has made the emblematic landscape of innocence not only real but accessible, encouraging the reader to make his own mystified journey in the belief that the object to which Nerval's language seems to refer really exists. Clearly the final narrator of *Sylvie* enjoys a perspective which "knows" the protagonist's earlier mystification, but as Proust realized, this in no way avoids the need for the narrative itinerary. The troubling duplicity of the text cannot be mastered, nor the error circumvented. The narrator at the end of *Sylvie* is aware that the vision of innocence has always been a product of a romantic imagination, but like Proust's story of Ruskin, he has written the text as an attempt to recoup the possibility of that lost vision. To the extent that the reader joins his hero's return to the "countryside of Sylvie," the distance to the vision is no longer ontological but temporal. The narrative may thus be seen, in part at least, as a strategic attempt to re-create a vision whose impossibility is explicitly acknowledged in the rest of the text.

In turning to the *Recherche*, we will be examining three major motifs which serve to call into question that vision to which Marcel and Gérard seem to be returning. Within the story of Marcel's progress toward his vocation and a clear sense of himself, these are the "countermovements" which continually undermine the possibility of knowing one's world clearly, or authenticating experience through an absolute standard of value, nobility. Throughout the novel, Marcel seems to approach a sense of identity, both his own and that of those around him (Gilberte, Swann, Odette, the Duchesse, Albertine), yet the judicial metaphor repeatedly calls into question whether or not such clear perception is at all possible. The final masks that Marcel finds at the last party of the novel would seem to deny that evidence ever resolves itself into a self-evident verdict. If we return, then, to the well-known themes of desire and the aristocracy, it will be to focus on them as vehicles of countermovement in Proust's text. In this context, Albertine eludes Marcel not simply as a woman eludes her jealous lover, but as a text escapes the reader's attempt to circumscribe it and know it completely. Similarly, when the aristocracy falls to sordid levels, toward the end of the novel, it destroys with it Marcel's hope for a guarantor of authenticity.

From Nerval, Proust has learned how to weave these movements—in the figure of the mystified hero and the knowledgeable narrator—into the deceptive first-person narrative. Nerval defied Sainte-Beuve by turning his life into part of his fiction, making it part of his strategy. As a reader of Nerval, Proust also feels he can travel to the world of *Sylvie*, but his entrance into the play of language in his critical essay signals a movement toward becoming a creator of fiction himself. The writer is the player who knows the emptiness of the object he seeks—an absence Nerval recognizes in his image of Rousseau's tomb, "la tombe où manquent les cendres de Rousseau."[12] Clearly, the only fruitful response to this void is to write the story of the journey. Proust travels to the Valois as he once did to Amiens and Venice, but his notion of idolatry is now far more sophisticated. Instead of expecting the voyage to yield the magic landscape of the fiction, the journey into Nerval's landscape will reveal fiction's deceptive nature. And the "misguided" itinerary will become the path tracing the reader's experience—even structuring the text itself.

3

The Reader as Judge

In order to understand their relation to his mature novel, it is necessary to consider Proust's essays on his predecessors from a point of view beyond the traditional sense of "influence." The essays on Ruskin and Nerval have rather taken the experience of reading as their central concern: they show Proust watching himself as a reader and thematizing the reading experience in preparation for organizing his own novel as a text *to be read*. In the discussion of the *Recherche* that follows, we will be examining various forms that the figure of the reader takes. He is first of all a kind of judge, an interpreter of the text—a singularly unhappy situation in this novel, as the metaphor of judging will reveal.

When Proust turned to parody in 1906 as a way of beginning to write fiction again, he introduced an important new theme into his repertoire, choosing as his subject a story of judgement as it might have been treated by various famous authors. He had been intensely interested in the Dreyfus Affair, and he imagined how these writers would describe the current trial of Lemoine, a lovable swindler who had coaxed a large sum of money out of the director of a large diamond concern with the claim that he could manufacture diamonds artificially. But the pastiches actually focus neither on the trial procedure nor on the criminal himself. Proust shows, rather, how this ostensible theme becomes merely the point of departure for the interests peculiar to each author. His "Balzac" describes the social relationships that become involved, "Saint-Simon" explains how the royal court may be tainted by the Affair, while "Renan" is concerned with the spirituality of Lemoine's attempt. Yet beyond these preoccupations, but not unrelated to the judicial motif, Proust's pastiches evoke the question that reflects Lemoine's own fraud: How can these essays seem to be what they are not, namely reports on the "Lemoine Affair" written by Balzac, Flaubert, the Goncourts, and the rest? That is, how do they intend their own reading? Because they are offered as counterfeits and to be appreciated must be read as self-conscious imitations, the pastiches continually pose the question of authorship and authenticity. They must be read as fakes which force the reader to ask how he is able to *judge* them and how he knows that they are deliberate masks, a kind of theater.

In similar fashion, Proust has written the *Recherche* in the first person, as though to suggest it were his life's story. His success at pseudo-autobiography may be gauged by the numerous misreadings which discuss interchangeably events in Proust's life and in Marcel's story.[1] More profoundly, Proust's use of the deceptive narrative "I," which refuses to distinguish him from his hero, inscribes in the text ultimate questions of its origin and its truth value: Who is speaking? Whose experiences are these? To what does this language refer? The reader is forced to be the kind of judge the jealous lover is: one unable to decide really whether it is even possible to *see* clearly enough to judge, or to judge clearly. He must determine at every moment on what level he can accept the evidence and how he can proceed to making a correct judgement. In order to appreciate the reader's difficulties with the text, we must examine the situation of an analogous figure in Proust's novel, the jealous lover, for whom these difficulties are greatly magnified. Love and desire, the motivation for his devoted reading of his mistress's signs, is one of the great themes of the *Recherche*. Swann's story is essentially of his love for Odette, while our sense of Charlus is formed to no small degree by his affairs with Jupien and Morel, and of course, much of the narrator's story traces his adventures with Gilberte, Albertine, and numerous fantasy figures. It is striking that in each of these affairs, jealousy turns the lover into an obsessive and fanatic reader of his mistress. Love is finally so intertwined in this novel with the need to penetrate appearances and to seize the truth about one's beloved that we are tempted to say that, for Proust, love means not having to tell the truth. Love creates the paradoxical attitude which allows Marcel to operate on the premise that Albertine is telling him the truth, even while his jealousy refuses to accept any of her explanations. During one fit of jealousy, when all his energies are aimed at catching his mistress in a lie, Marcel admits, "Je continuais à vivre sur l'hypothèse qui admettait pour vrai tout ce que me disait Albertine" (III, 346). Yet at the same time he is equally convinced that for fear of losing his love, Albertine will never reveal the truth of her past: "Il y avait une seule chose qu'elle ne ferait jamais plus pour moi . . . c'était précisément avouer" (III, 57). Jealousy, the driving force of love in the *Recherche*, forces the lover to act on contradictory premises: on the one hand, he believes that the evidence will reveal the truth, and on the other, he deeply suspects that whatever is revealed is intended to hide the truth. Between these poles, love weaves the story of the need to judge and the impossibility of judging.

More than just a story of love, *A la recherche* follows Marcel's repeated attempts to seize the secret of a remark, an impression, or a situation. This is an area where the excellent studies of Proust by Georges Poulet and Gilles Deleuze converge. For Poulet, this novel is a search for orientation and identity, and the question of finding out *who* one is, is equivalent to determining *where* one is. The existential Proustian search for temporal orientation is translatable, for Poulet, into a spatial attempt at localization:

Dans le premier de ces deux passages, il s'agit de personnes égarées dans l'espace externe, dans l'autre, d'un être perdu au milieu d'un espace intérieur. Mais dans un cas comme dans l'autre, l'événement essentiel est la reconnaissance du lieu. . . . Cette tâche porte un nom. Elle s'appelle *localisation*. Or, de même que l'esprit localise l'image remémorée dans la durée, il la localise dans l'espace.2

Deleuze sees the *Recherche* as Marcel's education in the reading of signs in the social world, in love, and in art. Both studies emphasize Marcel's need to penetrate appearances and to assimilate new impressions into an ever clearer grasp of the world through an increasingly refined ability to judge his experiences. As Proust himself seems to have done, Poulet and Deleuze see the *Recherche* as a gradual but constant progress toward the enlightenment of self-discovery and art. Another critic even borrows from Marcel the expression "rectification" to describe this movement of clarification and correction:

Le *Côté de Guermantes* s'insère dans le récit d'un itinéraire, comme la rectification des rêves et des illusions sur le monde.3

A close look at the theme of judgement in the novel, however, will reveal that a movement toward clarity is only half the story. As in the lover's ambivalent attitude toward evidence, there is a countercurrent in the *Recherche* of continued obfuscation and renewed error. And like Marcel in his irresolution, both directions are "true."

Judging is deliberately made a difficult endeavor in the *Recherche*, as the reader's path—and Marcel's—are strewn with deceptive impressions and invitations to misinterpretation. The history of Marcel's errors is being faithfully presented. Thematically, too, judging appears repeatedly as a dangerous and precarious activity. *La Prisonnière*, itself the record of Marcel's attempt to seize Albertine and know her completely, begins with a discussion of the hazards of trying to link an explanation of cause to a set of facts. Marcel's friend Bloch has traced the narrator's reluctance to leave his apartment at this time, a fact with which Bloch has long been acquainted, to a cause which Marcel has only just revealed:

Quand, beaucoup plus tard, [Bloch] apprit qu'Albertine habitait alors avec moi, comprenant que je l'avais cachée à tout le monde, il déclara qu'il voyait enfin la raison pour laquelle, à cette époque de ma vie, je ne voulais jamais sortir. Il se trompa. (III, 9)

The flow of the paragraph, following Bloch's careful logic, lets the reader down hard with the narrator's terse and definitive commentary. In taking the role of the judge here, Bloch is trying to locate the intentional center of Marcel's actions from which the manifest effects can be presumed to have arisen. The problem is that at best he can come up with a *plausible* solution, a *hypothetical* center which can "account for" the evidence. The actuality as Marcel knows it owes no allegiance to the limits of Bloch's imagination. Yet Marcel finds that the urge to explain actions through intentions was understandable, and even "fort excusable":

> [C]ar la réalité, même si elle est nécessaire, n'est pas complètement prévisible; ceux qui apprennent sur la vie d'un autre quelque détail exact en tirent aussitôt des conséquences qui ne le sont pas et voient dans le fait nouvellement découvert l'explication de choses qui précisément n'ont aucun rapport avec lui. (III, 9-10)

The jealous lover is an extreme case, of course, *driven* to judging his mistress, but repeatedly the narrative seems to insist that scarcely any judgement is defensible. From the obscurity of the Dreyfus Affair to the inscrutability of Albertine, the *Recherche* is filled with unsuccessful attempts at clear judgement. When at one point Marcel compares his situation as a lover to that of a trial judge, he describes a man forced by his legal position to make a decision which, although it affects life and death, is always based on conflicting evidence and inadequate testimony:

> J'en serais réduit pour toujours, comme un juge, à tirer des conclusions incertaines d'imprudences de langage qui n'étaient peut-être pas inexplicables sans avoir recours à la culpabilité. (III, 57-58)

Nothing could be further from the classical image of Justice than the position to which Marcel is "reduced." That figure, scales in hand and blindfolded, weighs impartially and sees clearly, blind to prejudice and circumstance— embodying the full possibility of judging fairly. But Marcel and Swann are reluctant judges placed in an impossible position. Already early on in the novel, Marcel has shown that a person we see is less a definite object than a subjective construct, expressing rather our lack of imagination. The Swann who frequented the highest levels of society is so inconceivable to Marcel's family because they have allowed their narrow impression to fill his whole being:

> Nous remplissons l'apparence physique de l'être que nous voyons de toutes les notions que nous avons sur lui . . . [si parfaitement] que chaque fois que nous voyons ce visage . . . ce sont ces notions que nous retrouvons. . . . (I, 19)

The person we know is not "un tout matériellement constitué, identique pour tout le monde et dont chacun n'a qu'à aller prendre connaissance" (I, 19), but the focus of a necessary and inescapable act of interpretation. The similarity to a difficult text whose meaning lies only in our reading is confirmed by a passage we recall from one of Proust's essays on Ruskin. Reading becomes a dangerous temptation, he warned, when the text presents itself as a kind of given, substituting itself for the necessary act of interpretation so that truth appears "comme une chose matérielle" available in books for the mere taking, "comme un miel tout préparé par les autres" (*CSB*, pp. 180-81).

The difficulty of successfully tracing the path from evidence to causes is illustrated in profuse examples of misguided premises, deceptive appearances, and the willingness to reach conclusions based on insufficient information. Charlus's reputation among the bourgeoisie exemplifies one aspect of the problem: to the bourgeois social world his name is anathema, for he is known as a sexual pervert there. Since they are unaware of his place in the highest aristocracy, they conclude that his sexual excesses are the reason for his exclusion from their own social ranks. In fact, Marcel tells us, he is probably being confused with a certain Comte Leblois de Charlus, of no relation, who was once arrested in a famous police raid, but "peut-être par erreur" (II, 903). The bourgeoisie, who know him least, stumble on the "truth" about Charlus through a series of erroneous suppositions, mistaken identities, misinformation, and indefensible logic. But the most telling failures of judgement, calling into question the entire possibility of making a successful judgement, occur where a lover is trying to discover the secrets of his mistress, to control her by knowing all about her.

La Prisonnière, the story of Albertine's captivity, describes the most elaborate attempt to circumscribe the evidence completely, and it offers perhaps the clearest failures of judgement. The "truth" about Albertine and the control Marcel seeks continue to elude his every strategy. His interest itself—like Swann's love for Odette—is founded on an unsuspected falsehood, on Albertine's claim that she was practically raised by Mlle Vinteuil's friend whom Marcel knows to be a lesbian. His subsequent efforts at "capturing" her are aimed at discovering the truth of her past and preventing possible future lesbian activities. In this revelation as in others, Marcel later finds he was further from the truth after Albertine's remark than before, as she was lying to impress him. He laments that, "Nous pouvons avoir roulé toutes les idées possibles, la vérité n'y est jamais entrée" (II, 1114). Albertine has achieved her desired effect, but "par un autre chemin que celui qu'elle avait voulu prendre" (III, 337), by a path, that is, entirely unimaginable to her.

The lesbianism Marcel suspects is itself a physical analogue of his ignorance of Albertine; it is a void beyond his ability to know, like the emptiness before which her lies place him. To a man, lesbianism is the quintessential *lacune*: physically, it defies his imagination by its lack of visible organs, and it eludes his experience by excluding him totally. Marcel remarks in a reflective moment, "Cet amour entre femmes était quelque chose de trop inconnu, dont rien ne permettait d'imaginer avec certitude, avec justesse, les plaisirs, la qualité" (III, 385). He finds himself intrigued—and defeated—by the elusiveness of Albertine's lies, just as he is attracted and repelled by her lesbianism; each is the flaw, the missing link in the whole which guarantees the impossibility of capture. The story of the jealous lover is that of his attempt to defeat the elusiveness of these lies, these signs which Deleuze has said address us only "en nous cachant ce qu'ils expriment."[4] In his affair with Odette, Swann is driven to find out whether, as he suspects, Forcheville was hiding in her apartment on the evening she turned him away. His love grows out of this central uncertainty, as Marcel's love grows from the suspicion of Albertine's lesbianism. The lover's attempt to possess his mistress is parallel to his desire to master the language of *mensonge* which eludes him. He is constrained to examine all her statements and plans and to compare her stories carefully, hoping to surprise the truth in between the contradictions of her lies, and to reestablish the control over her which assures fidelity. Ironically, the jealous lover is forced into the role of "judge" of his mistress by the certainty of her guilt. His jealous desire builds itself around an invisible center which he can never penetrate and around which his mistress weaves a web of lies. Marcel laments, "[Albertine] causait mes maux comme une divinité qui reste invisible" (III, 152); the source of these lies remaining invisible, their intention will necessarily always elude him.

These lies, real and imagined, are what make the lover's task extraordinarily difficult: he is defeated by the same void of *mensonge* which incites his quest. Jealousy, Marcel discovers, struggles inside a vacuum, deprived of all sure points of reference. In its structure as well as in its objective, "la jalousie se débat dans le vide" (III, 147). It becomes increasingly difficult to distinguish between "true" evidence and disguise. Marcel is convinced that Albertine will never admit her guilt, yet the nature of his suspicion makes it impossible for her ever to prove her innocence: the code of interpretation is determining the message. The figure of the jealous lover even becomes a parody of Justice, for it is now "la jalousie qui a un bandeau sur les yeux" (III, 151). Nevertheless, it seems to Marcel that there *once* was a time when he might have learned the definitive truth about Albertine's past, and he regrets not having done so: "C'est quand elle ne soupçonnait pas encore que j'étais jaloux d'elle, que j'aurais dû lui demander ce que je voulais savoir" (III, 58). When they were casual friends, she spoke freely of herself, but with their new relationship, she grew reluctant to risk losing his interest by revealing too much. By this point, of course, Marcel can no longer recall what she revealed:

> Je me souvenais; j'avais connu une première Albertine, puis brusquement elle avait été changée en une autre, l'actuelle. Et le changement, je n'en pouvais rendre responsable que moi-même. Tout ce qu'elle m'eût avoué facilement, puis volontiers, quand nous étions de bons camarades, avait cessé de s'épandre dès qu'elle avait cru que je l'aimais. (III, 57)

Marcel is hypothesizing an ideal moment when he already knew what was significant *and* found it available to him, like the reader of a complex novel who would know at once what to make of the early clues whose significance emerges only upon rereading. Such revelations are never offered the jealous lover "facilement." The conviction that Albertine is concealing crucial facts about herself turns all her words into *camouflage* for Marcel. In the present, where judgement is no longer a possibility, her denials are available to him only as further proofs of her guilt:

> Albertine pouvait me nier ses trahisons particulières; par des mots qui lui échappaient, plus forts que les déclarations contraires, par ces regards seuls, elle avait fait l'aveu de ce qu'elle avait voulu cacher. (III, 150)

Knowing she is lying, however, only shows him his ignorance without bringing him closer to the truth. If there were a time when judgement was possible, it was when Marcel could still believe Albertine's statements and receive them as evidence. But this was when he was not yet suspicious of her, when her language could be interpreted literally. The time when her language was innocent, not yet corrupted by the need to deceive, is a different time completely, when Marcel was not yet interested in Albertine. But she was a different person for him then, not yet invested with interest and elaborated by his imagination, just as "la femme qui est partie n'est plus la même que celle qui était là" (III, 425). And the "pastness" of this era of possibility is perhaps a metaphor for this difference. With its passing, not only does the truth about Albertine and her past vanish, but the entire possibility of seeing clearly and of receiving direct revelation is gone for Marcel—lost irretrievably in the past. He cannot help feeling defeated in the very inception of his project: "Depuis ce jour-là, elle m'avait tout caché" (III, 57). He finds himself forced to take the role of judge just when the possibility of judging seems to have disappeared.

The question implicit in Marcel's investigations is whether direct revelation was ever possible, or language ever innocent. Like a judge faced with a mass of confusing and contradictory evidence, the lover must construct his own story of his mistress. A judge is not an omniscient narrator, however, but rather like a storyteller who must assemble the elements of his story, creating it from the evidence.[5] A judge must interpret the evidence by deciding which facts are significant and defining them for the purpose of forming them into the "legal fiction" of the guilty party. His picture of the truth is invariably clearer than the evidence present: ignorance expresses itself with characteristically greater assurance than knowledge. The meaningful constellation of the facts which results allows the evidence—now linked causally—to appear to emanate from an intentional center. The judge can now "discover" retroactively in that evidence the motivation and causality which he seeks—and which his constellation has already inscribed into it. Only in retrospect does the whole become self-evident: the source of the evidence can now be found in its story, much as the essence of a book is afterwards discovered in its preface—"Préfaces, c'est-à-dire pages écrites après . . ." (III, 160).

Bloch and Marcel are also assembling fragments of evidence into a story whose significance exists *for them*, while the narrative repeatedly reveals the ability of reality to elude and deceive this process. Nevertheless, the lover persistently refuses to accept the subjective and tentative nature of these constructs. Marcel still hopes to meet the ideal figure who could tell him literally *all* about Albertine, even as he realizes the fictionality of such a person:

> Les romanciers prétendent souvent dans une introduction qu'en voyageant dans un pays ils ont rencontré quelqu'un qui leur a raconté la vie d'une personne. Ils laissent alors la parole à cet ami de rencontre, et le récit qu'il leur fait c'est précisément leur roman. . . . Combien nous voudrions quand nous aimons . . . trouver un tel narrateur informé! (III, 551)

The similarity is once again apparent between this temptation and the one Proust has warned against in "Sur la lecture." He insists that the truth of a work must be discovered in ourselves: the hope of finding the secret document which will finally reveal the whole truth is just an escape:

> Quel bonheur, quel repos pour un esprit fatigué de chercher la vérité en lui-même de se dire qu'elle est située hors de lui, aux feuillets d'un in-folio jalousement conservé dans un couvent de Hollande, et que si, pour arriver jusqu'à elle, il faut se donner de la peine, cette peine sera toute matérielle, ne sera pour la pensée qu'un délassement plein de charme. (*CSB*, p. 181)

Marcel's problem, of course, is that such a person may not exist, that there may be *no* privileged, "true" text, and that the only answer to his search lies in the fiction that he can provide. Yet in the terms that Proust used to discuss Nerval, this search must be *sincère*, that is, it must take as its premise the possibility of knowing the truth clearly. A key paradigm of this search in the *Recherche*—and of its disappointment—is the Dreyfus Affair. Interests of honor, deceit, and political gain have woven an intricate web of side issues and complications around the Affair. As in the *Pastiches*, these issues which bear only indirectly on Dreyfus have reduced the man and his alleged crime to mere pretexts. Nevertheless, despite the sense that these complications have gained an importance far exceeding Dreyfus or his actions, all the principals in the Affair continue to act as though their attentions are directed solely toward the literal Dreyfus, the ostensible center of the proceedings. The naive members of the public imagine that the Affair still rotates around Dreyfus' guilt or innocence. The project is strikingly similar to an idolatrous reading: as though the nature of a complex metaphor were to be found in its literal point of departure. Those outside governmental and judicial circles accept the terms of the Dreyfus debate literally, believing that the simple fact of the matter can be learned, the issues resolved and laid to rest. When Bloch interrogates Norpois, he reveals the conviction on the periphery that those at the center of the storm *must* know the true facts of the case:

> Mais où Bloch se trompait, c'est quand il croyait que M. de Norpois . . . eût pu, s'il l'avait voulu, lui dire la vérité sur le rôle d'Henry, de Picquart, de du Paty de Clam, sur tous les points de l'affaire. La vérité, en effet, sur toutes ces choses, Bloch ne pouvait douter que M. de Norpois la connût. Comment l'aurait-il ignorée puisqu'il connaissait les ministres? (II, 241)

This attitude is a denial of the complexity of language, insisting that the complication of the metaphor can be dispensed with. It expresses a notion of truth as unique, simple, material, and knowable, insisting there exists at the "center" the essential and clear truth, the source of all causality, just as there must exist a witness who can tell all about our mistress. This secret truth must be able completely to explain (away) the disturbing complexity of the Dreyfus Affair:

> Certes, Bloch pensait que la vérité politique peut être approximativement reconstituée par les cerveaux les plus lucides, mais il s'imaginait, tout comme le gros du public, qu'elle habite toujours, indiscutable et matérielle, le dossier secret du président de la république. . . . Or, même quand la vérité politique comporte des documents, il est rare que ceux-ci aient plus que la valeur d'un cliché radioscopique où le vulgaire croit que la maladie du patient s'inscrit en toutes lettres, tandis qu'en fait, ce cliché fournit un simple élément d'appréciation qui se joindra à beaucoup d'autres sur lesquels s'appliquera le raisonnement du médecin et d'où il tirera son diagnostique. (II, 241-42)

These are denials of the act of diagnosis, refusals of interpretation. Bloch and the others are insisting that the truth can be known im-mediately, lucid and *indiscutable*, but the figure of the X-ray picture reveals that even transparence is inadequate: the evidence is never self-evident and requires always a return to an interpretive act. To those whom Bloch imagines at the center, the center appears to be elsewhere; it is always others who are privy to the crucial information.

In view of the persistence of error and the denial of simple truth, readers of Proust must beware of critics who would explain away error through the progress of the narrator. Gaëtan Picon discards an essential element of the narrative when he "annuls" the illusory. Roger Shattuck makes a similar mistake by overexpanding his optical metaphor; he sees the novel as the progressive refinement of Marcel's "binoculars" to correct the distortions through which he sees the world. "Rays of light can be refracted or reflected into an image of their source,"[6] he states, implying that Proust uses various literary techniques the way astronomers use a telescope, to correct for the inadequacy of Marcel's vision and to bring him beyond his error so he can find the true meaning of the evidence. But as Shattuck must realize, Marcel's problem is epistemological; at its root lies not a distortion to be corrected, but an optical illusion, that is, a structure of perception which cannot be "corrected for." It can, however, be explained away by a metaphor which fails to accept "error" as an essential part of Marcel's itinerary.

Bloch, of course, believes that this clear truth exists, but it is always kept from him for some undeniably essential reason: diplomatic discretion, national security, insufficient penetration. Marcel, too, needs to believe he will reach the truth about Albertine, although it is especially agonizing to feel himself a mystified spectator regarding his mistress, for in the eyes of others, he must certainly appear to occupy the privileged center of her life. Marcel knows the hopelessness of his attempts to know Albertine, "Pourtant, à des étrangers il eût dû sembler que personne autant que moi ne pouvait connaître sa vie" (III, 551). Nevertheless, he persists in his search for that "narrateur informé": "Et certes il existe" (III, 551). We hear in this passage the kind of desperate hope with which Gérard assured himself that his pastoral dream could be found again in the real world. Marcel vindicates the authenticity of his quest with this conviction, and surely part of the woman's attraction lies in her ability to cultivate the illusion of success. He confesses his dilemma, "Cet être-là existe toujours . . . mais nous ne le rencontrons jamais," and returns to the image of the privileged figure near the center of a state secret: "C'est ainsi que l'on croit que l'ami d'un ministre doit savoir la vérité sur certaines affaires" (III, 551).

Failing to find the essential witness or the perfect piece of evidence, the jealous lover must exploit what evidence he can reach, orienting it and determining its *sens*, much as Marcel, lying awake in his bedroom, must try to figure out where he is, "en rapprochant les circonstances" (I, 6). He has to develop a strategy to surprise the truth. Swann, for example, presupposes that truth is of an essentially different quality from falsehood, enabling him to make the crucial distinction. When Odette lies to him, he imagines he can come closer to the concealed fact by "opening up" her lies to confirm his suspicions. The logic involved is simple: "En voyant Odette lui faire ainsi le signe que c'était faux, Swann comprit que c'était peut-être vrai" (I, 362). Since truth corresponds to its intention (unlike a lie, which is only intended to conceal or disguise the truth), both Marcel and Swann believe they can discover it even swathed in a tissue of deceptive gestures. When Odette, hoping to make her stories more credible, introduces a fragment of truth, that grain is what betrays her, for the "angles" of intention of "la Vérité" differentiate it from the matrix of lies:

> Certes quand Odette venait de faire quelque chose qu'elle ne voulait pas révéler, elle le cachait bien au fond d'elle-même. Mais dès qu'elle se trouvait en présence de celui à qui elle voulait mentir, un trouble la prenait . . . elle ne trouvait plus dans sa tête que le vide. (I, 278)

Finding to fill this blank only that which she would hide, Odette takes just a piece of it, assuring herself that "Ça du moins, c'est vrai . . . ce n'est toujours pas ça qui me trahira." But therein the narrator finds her mistake (in his triumphant manner):

> Elle se trompait, c'était cela qui la trahissait, elle ne se rendait pas compte que ce détail vrai avait des angles qui ne pouvait s'emboîter que dans les détails contigus du fait vrai dont elle l'avait arbitrairement détaché et qui, quels que fussent les détails inventés entre lesquels elle le placerait, révéleraient toujours par la matière excédente et les vides non remplis, que ce n'était pas d'entre ceux-là qu'il venait. (I, 278)

Marcel assumes that the fiction that replaces the emptiness of the lie gives itself away. He therefore enjoys that same advantage over Albertine: he can catch her lying from the "accent" that distinguishes the *mensonge*. At other times, she reveals herself by an innocence too exaggerated to be believed. Like the excessive nonchalance Charlus displays while spying on Saint-Loup, these lies expose themselves by "une exagération agressive." As their object is to conceal (camouflage) rather than reveal (message), to Marcel's logic they betray themselves by their different intention: the strange ease in Charlus shows Marcel his desire *not* to be noticed (I, 752). Once he thinks he understands the logic and code of Albertine's lies, Marcel believes it a simple matter to decipher the meaning of her words. Like Swann, he will simply read them "à rebours":

> Parfois l'écriture où je déchiffrais les mensonges d'Albertine sans être idéographique, avait simplement besoin d'être lue à rebours; c'est ainsi que ce soir elle m'avait lancé d'un air négligent ce message destiné à passer presque inaperçue: "Il serait possible que j'aille demain chez les Verdurin, je ne sais pas du tout si j'irai, je n'en ai guère envie." Anagramme enfantin de cet aveu: "J'irai demain chez les Verdurin, c'est absolument certain, car j'y attache une extrême importance." (III, 90-91)

This decoding process has its own pitfalls; though Marcel may sense the lie, the reversing of Albertine's childish anagrams brings him no closer to the truth. On the contrary, the language of deception shows itself to be dialectical: when Albertine perceives that Marcel will accept only statements which are *vraisemblables*, she learns to defeat his logic by lying with no other intention than to be plausible. She tells him of meeting Bergotte one evening, and Marcel has no grounds for doubting the authenticity of their conversation. When he afterward learns of Bergotte's death on that day, he concludes that his mistress must have been the last to see him alive, and he berates the newspapers for their imprecision in reporting him dead already by late afternoon. Only much later does he discover that Albertine's story was a pure fiction, probably fashioned to cover up some adventure she wished to hide, but which he had no reason at all to suspect. Her lie was effective because it appeared unmotivated, and it was so completely fictive that it gave no grounds for suspicion:

> [J]e n'appris que bien plus tard l'art charmant qu'elle avait de mentir avec simplicité. Ce qu'elle disait, ce qu'elle avouait avait tellement les mêmes caractères que les formes de l'évidence . . . qu'elle semait ainsi dans les intervalles de sa vie les épisodes d'une autre vie dont je ne soupçonnais pas alors la fausseté. (III, 189)

Some of Albertine's lies leave no trace of their intention, so Marcel is unprepared to suspect her statements. His entire method is undermined, therefore, by the inability to doubt extensively enough. At times in answer to a question from him, Albertine will admit having met the person and having exchanged a few insignificant words, but will insist that "il n'y a jamais rien eu entre nous." Marcel finds himself completely at a loss, since his question was a trial and he knows Albertine is lying:

> Or Albertine n'avait même pas rencontré cette personne, pour la bonne raison que celle-ci n'était pas venue à Paris depuis deux mois. Mais mon amie trouvait que nier complètement était peu vraisemblable. D'où cette courte rencontre fictive, dite si simplement que je voyais la dame s'arrêter, lui dire bonjour, faire quelques pas avec elle. (III, 189)

He can only admire the incredible verisimilitude of her fiction, which turns out to be even more compelling than the truth. Because her fiction is created out of a void and possesses only appearance, its evidence of existence must be more convincing than details which arise from a "real" existence. In their moments of certitude, Marcel and Swann feel sure this striving for realistic appearance will betray the *mensonge*, but more often they are confronted by the limitations of their imagination and by their inability to remain radically critical of *all* evidence.

Albertine replaces a confession of her adventures with stories about herself and thus teaches Marcel a lesson in the nature of fiction. What is so terribly effective about her lies is that they offer him only the gaping void of his ignorance. Even discovered, the lie reveals only a negative truth: that Albertine is lying. The lover is presented with a difficult choice: facing the emptiness of his ignorance or accepting the fiction which convincingly replaces that void. Marcel's experiences with Albertine's lies, as a closer examination of her "textuality" will reveal, are analogous to a reader's attempt to master a text. The Albertine which Marcel comes to penetrate is always a fiction, a reading of the evidence she offers, with only an incidental relationship to whatever she is concealing behind her lies. But in another sense, this concealment and evasion are at least as "true" of Albertine as is her lesbianism.

Looking again at the *Pastiches*, it will be seen that Lemoine's crime, for many of the spectators, is not his defrauding the diamond merchant De Beers, but his inability to fulfill the fantastic *possibilities* he had evoked. His crime was that he could not in fact make diamonds and sustain the dreams of the common people. Flaubert's sad onlookers ask themselves,

> [P]ourquoi n'avait-il pas dit vrai, fabriqué du diamant, divulgué son invention? Tous, et jusqu'au plus pauvre, auraient su—c'était certain—en tirer des millions. (*CSB*, p. 14)

"Flaubert" comments that those people hated Lemoine most, with a violence characteristic of regret, who were defrauded not of their money, but of their dreams. The "Renan" sketch makes the distinction even clearer between this spiritual lack and the grasp of vulgar literalism:

> Si Lemoine avait réellement fabriqué du diamant, il eût sans doute contenté par là, dans une certaine mesure, ce matérialisme grossier [de l'humanité] ... il n'eût pas donné aux âmes éprises d'idéal cet élément d'exquise spiritualité. (*CSB*, p. 31)

Most remarkable about Lemoine, as about any confidence man, is his climactic *failure* to produce the goods—and his corresponding success at producing illusions. Lemoine has had a far more powerful effect with no diamonds in his pocket than he might have had, were he simply a successful chemical engineer.

As a great creator of illusion, Proust is greatly interested in the process and effect of fiction. Albertine demonstrates his fascination with the ability of the *mensonge* to create an absence which no actuality can fill. Much of Proust's admiration for Balzac is directed toward that novelist's ability not only to write superb fiction himself but to create characters who are themselves artists of illusion. The characters from the *Comédie humaine* named repeatedly by Proust are those who are able to weave an exquisite and supremely effective fiction: Lucien de Rubempré, Vautrin, and most of all, that precursor of Odette de Crécy, Diane de Cadignan. The dress that the Princesse de Cadignan wears to seduce d'Arthez, like that of Giotto's *Charité*, is an emblem of particular attraction for Proust, and one to which he returned several times. In the *Recherche*, Marcel joins Charlus in idolatrous admiration of Albertine's dress, "une harmonieuse combinaison de couleurs grises, comme celle de Diane de Cadignan" (II, 1055). The use of the dress is clearly ironic, for Marcel is the unwitting subject of Albertine's charms, an unselfconscious d'Arthez committing the error of idolatry which Proust attacked, using the same example, in his preface to Ruskin's *Bible d'Amiens*. If Proust admires her "dress," it is as a masterpiece of intention, embodying the Princesse's attempt to create a perfect illusion for d'Arthez. She succeeds because the art of her dress so completely conceals its artifice: the result of such careful preparation and strategy is a vision of simplicity. In Balzac's own description, the naturalness of its appearance defies Science:

> Il était impossible au physionomiste le plus habile d'imaginer des calculs et de la décision sous cette inouïe délicatesse de traits. . . . Elle arriva de bonne heure, afin de se trouver posée sur la causeuse, au coin du feu, près de Mme d'Espard, comme elle voulait être vue dans une de ces attitudes où la science est cachée sous un naturel exquis.[7]

Proust sees the dress as the incarnation of the fictional project, able to cover its traces and manifest itself as pure artlessness. "Une femme nue," Balzac cautions admiringly, "serait moins dangereuse que ne l'est une jupe si savamment étalée, qui couvre tout et met tout en lumière à la fois."[8] What chance has a jealous lover before a fiction more real-seeming than reality, which can captivate because, like the song of the Sirens, it seems to bring an illusion within reach, making the ideal a real possibility?

The lover feels closer to his impossible objective, for desire finds a response in fiction that it cannot find in reality, as Marcel learns:

> Et nous pensons avec plus de joie à une vie où—à condition que nous écartions pour un instant de notre pensée le petit obstacle accidentel et particulier qui nous empêche personnellement de le faire—nous pouvons nous imaginer l'assouvissant. (I, 712)

The jealous lover, blinded by desire—for the woman and for the truth (that is, the mastery) of her—allows himself always to be convinced that the obstacle keeping him from the object of his desire is only small and accidental. The woman's fiction makes this continuous deception possible by seeming to place the desired object almost within reach. The Princesse de Cadignan wins d'Arthez by turning herself into a work of art, in order to create the illusion of a perfect love affair. When Balzac describes her language, he is portraying the language of fiction:

> Dans cette phrase, tout entre d'Arthez et la Princesse était vague comme une promesse, doux comme une espérance, et néanmoins certain comme un droit. Avouons-le? ces sortes de grandeurs n'appartiennent qu'à ces illustres et sublimes trompeuses.[9]

Fiction throws the reader-lover between the void of *mensonge* and the desired object: the attempt at judgement fails because it seeks to defeat the "in-betweenness" of the moment by resolving the *difference* into a unique *sens*. Albertine is teaching Marcel a lesson in the nature of fiction, and revealing the attempt to seize the elusive image through its concrete, literal presence as the kind of idolatry Proust found both in Ruskin and in his own reading of

Ruskin. The idolatrous project appears in all of Marcel's attempts at appropriation—of the clear truth about Albertine, of the essence of the aristocracy, or of the literary beauty of Balbec. As the most compelling creator of illusion, Albertine demonstrates to Marcel the elusiveness of the text-object and the futility of trying to capture it. She remains an invisible fury because the center of the evidence she presents can never be located in reality. His failure to capture her—indeed, he becomes rather her prisoner—is part of the countercurrent running through the *Recherche* which we are emphasizing. In counterpoint to Marcel's apparent progress toward a clearer grasp of his world and his vocation, this "other" movement continually puts into question the entire possibility of seeing clearly and knowing enough to judge the meaning and direction of experience.

Albertine is able to maintain Marcel's interest, and it remains to examine how she is able to succeed. She manages to exploit the forceful *particularity* of fiction which obliterates history. She is able to create an illusion which answers to the frustration of Marcel's search, an illusion which convinces him each time that "the other images were merely illusion, but this is real." Thus, although Marcel knows the most intimate details of Swann's experience, he falls into the same traps, even reenacting Swann's story. Like a reader who is always reading a text for the first time, Marcel is so preoccupied with one level of meaning that he cannot sense other clues which always surprise him. In *La Prisonnière*, we find Marcel caught time and again between his image of a woman and the instances of her presence. As with Gilberte, he discovers he can love Albertine only when she is absent:

> [C]es joies, loin de les devoir à Albertine . . . que j'avais la sensation nette de ne pas aimer, je les goûtais au contraire pendant qu'Albertine n'était pas auprès de moi. (III, 12)

He is caught between the tiny, insignificant pieces of evidence and the whole essence of his mistress which may yet be revealed by such a small detail. We must see why Marcel is necessarily caught up in the attempt to possess himself of the unknown, that "other" quality in the woman he desires. The tone of the search is surely set when he approaches Albertine's room for the first time, in Balbec, promising himself, "J'allais savoir l'odeur, le goût qu'avait ce fruit inconnu" (I, 934).

4

The Textuality of Albertine

Toward the end of his essay on Nerval, Proust tries to clarify the "troubled pleasure" of the work of fiction; it is an indirect effect of the illusion produced, an evocation:

> Mais on ne nous rend pas le trouble que nous donne notre maîtresse en parlant de l'amour, mais en disant ces petites choses qui peuvent l'évoquer, le tissu de sa robe, son prénom. (*CSB*, p. 241)

The text works indirectly *by way of* the mistress's dress, and because it constitutes itself around the *absence* of the desired object, the text is always able to elude the reader's attempt to master it. Proust's image here suggests that the motif of desire, like that of the voyage, will be one of the principal directions for Marcel's projected appropriation of his world. Like *Sylvie*, Proust's text will evoke the illusion that a fictional element can be translated to another plane and seized in its empirical form. Marcel will travel to Balbec as Gérard returned idolatrously to the Valois, and he will imagine possessing a peasant girl who will offer him the essence of the Méséglise countryside as Gérard hoped to possess his childhood innocence in the girl Sylvie. But the text shows itself always to be elsewhere, no matter where the pursuer travels; the troubled pleasure is his sense of the disjunctive realities which seem to merge in the name:

> Mais notre plaisir est fait de trouble. La grâce mesurée du paysage en est la matière, mais il va au-delà. Cet au-delà est indéfinissable. Il sera un jour chez Gérard la folie. En attendant il n'a rien de mesuré, de bien français. (*CSB*, p. 240)

The countryside is only the *form* of the dream; the fantasized conquest of the girl and the assertive return to the place are different versions of the idolatrous textual project, the attempt to go outside the text and seize it elsewhere. This chapter will suggest that Albertine is not merely a psychologically "real" woman, but that she exists also as a *text*—a text which constantly eludes Marcel.[1] In the realm of desire, this urge to fulfill the textual illusion in reality

The Textuality of Albertine 61

becomes the attempt to possess the woman seen from a distance. Paraphrasing Proust on Nerval, we might say that "this troubled feeling will one day become Marcel's quest for Albertine." The *trouble* is the elusiveness at the center of his search for the "real" Albertine, for Balbec, for Venice—or even for his true vocation as a writer.

Marcel, as Albertine's jealous lover, finds himself a "judge" of his mistress, an interpreter standing on the periphery trying to locate the center of her being. Details seem only to lead him astray, rather than to her essence. Gaëtan Picon has noticed with discomfort the tendency in Proust's novel for the particular to merge into the general. Even the most individualized of his characters, in Picon's view, do not escape the sweeping vision which sees them as representatives of their "type":

> Les plus nettement particularisés, les plus présents des personnages n'échappent pas à cette vision qui les traverse et les annule. Qu'est M. de Charlus? Le composé de sa race et de son vice. Qu'est Swann? Bien des choses, sans doute, mais à la fin, son attitude devant l'affaire Dreyfus prouve qu'il est aussi un représentant de sa race—un Juif.[2]

Whether or not this generalization "annuls" the individual remains to be seen, but Picon's remark takes note of an area of concern which is also part of the narrator's difficulty in judging. Marcel never quite feels he is coming into contact with actual reality. Either he cannot find an individual person or object which sufficiently embodies its image, or he is blocked from the general idea by details which preoccupy him. He can never be convinced he has met a real Guermantes, for those he encounters fail to come up to his sense of who they *should* be, that is, who they were for him before he met them. When he has finally befriended the Guermantes, once the incarnation for him of the ultimate in nobility, he finds the actual members of that family so very different from his image of them that they have only the name in common.[3]

Marcel's difficulty arises perhaps from "une nécessité de prendre à la lettre ce qu'on me dit"[4] and from his reluctance to accept any concrete manifestation of the name as sufficient incarnation of the myth. The inability of reality to embody all the imagination has invested in it is especially characteristic of Marcel's sexual adventures. As he once tried to capture Balbec by possessing Albertine, he later tries to retrieve Albertine in Andrée. The mystification of desire expresses itself through the two central and interrelated illusions of the woman and the journey:

> Mais enfin, j'avais autrefois l'illusion de ressaisir Balbec, quand, à Paris, Albertine venait me voir et que je la tenais dans mes bras: de même que je prenais un contact, bien étroit et furtif d'ailleurs, avec la vie d'Albertine . . . quand j'embrassais une ouvrière. (III, 552)

There is a *jeu* of substitutions occurring here whereby a new object of desire is allowed to replace another when the first is beyond reach or beneath interest:

> Andrée, ces autres femmes, tout cela par rapport à Albertine—comme Albertine avait été elle-même par rapport à Balbec—étaient de ces substituts de plaisirs se remplaçant l'un l'autre en dégradation successive, qui nous permettent de nous passer de celui que nous ne pouvons atteindre, voyage à Balbec ou amour d'Albertine ... [et qui] font de notre vie comme une suite de zones concentriques, contiguës, harmoniques et dégradées, autour d'un désir premier. (III, 552)

The problem of judgement is infinitely complicated by the loss of a true center here, by this continual disappearance of the original evidence. Desire cooperates with fiction by always placing its object one step beyond reach. The original, the object of the "désir premier," is constantly being replaced by an intermediary, a substitute which is never quite the true object of desire. Yet in theory at least, Marcel, like Swann, refuses the substitution of a sure conquest for an inaccessible woman as "une lâche abdication" which cheats desire of the specificity of its origins. Love, for Marcel, is one of the ways of moving out of oneself and making real contact with the world. The peasant girl he imagines coming to him from Roussainville is necessarily and intimately attached to the landscape; meeting her in Paris would amount to fraud, "c'eût été recevoir des coquillages que je n'aurais pas vus sur la plage," for he imagines she will offer him a privileged contact "d'approcher de plus près ... la saveur profonde du pays" (I, 157). The possibility of substituting one woman for another turns love from an intense, personal thrust toward the world into a self-indulgent, narcissistic abstraction:

> [J]'étais pour longtemps encore à l'âge où l'on n'a pas encore abstrait ce plaisir de la possession des femmes différentes avec lesquelles on l'a goûté, où on ne l'a pas réduit à une notion générale qui les fait considérer dès lors comme les instruments interchangeables d'un plaisir toujours identique. (I, 157)

Substitution is possible only because each desire is *sincère*, captivating the desirer, so that each seems in fact "un désir premier." The project which turns Albertine into "la prisonnière" can be seen as one great attempt to solve the problem of preserving the ability of the incarnation to embody the significance of the image while still offering an object to judgement and desire.

The imprisonment of Albertine in his apartment is Marcel's attempt to capture the "être de fuite" which she has been for him since he first saw her. Even before he had heard her name, she was one of the ephemeral "jeunes filles en fleurs," a young cyclist "sans cesse en fuite sur sa bicyclette" (III, 371) whose glance perhaps showed her more readily seducible than the others. The band of young girls are a combination of distance and flight, an image of uncapturable *fraîcheur* like the water of the Vivonne. At their age, in this stage of "solidification incomplète," the adolescent girls are an emblem of pure suggestiveness to Marcel, evoking only the possibilities of what they may become. They precipitate a focus of the desire he feels which is still in search of its object:

> J'étais dans une de ces périodes de la jeunesse, dépourvues d'un amour particulier . . . —on désire, on cherche, on voit la Beauté. Qu'un seul trait réel—le peu qu'on distingue d'une femme vue de loin, ou de dos—nous permette de projeter la Beauté devant nous. (I, 787)

As suggestion, the girls are one part of a metaphor whose incompleteness incites Marcel's imagination to elaborate an image around the minute—but real—center they present. Albertine also participates in this distance and inaccessibility; she will later seem inscrutable to him because of her lesbian interests, but from the very first she has attracted Marcel by virtue of her membership in the exclusive little band:

> Ni parmi les actrices, ou les paysannes, ou les demoiselles de pensionnat religieux, je n'avais rien vu d'aussi beau, imprégné d'autant d'inconnu, aussi inestimablement précieux, aussi vraisemblablement inaccessible. (I, 797)

Already here, Marcel's desire is aroused by the unknowability at the center of their group: their appearance from a distance offers him only a sense of the inestimable "bonheur inconnu" of knowing them. Their constant presence along the beach is played against their lively flight from all attempts to meet or know them. Albertine excites him most of all by her ideal combination of suggestiveness and inaccessibility, by the gleam in her eyes that is "irréalisable, mais enivrant":

> Je savais que je ne posséderais pas cette jeune cycliste, si je ne possédais aussi ce qu'il y avait dans ses yeux. Et c'était par conséquent toute sa vie qui m'inspirait du désir; désir douloureux, parce que je le sentais irréalisable, mais enivrant. . . . (I, 794)

Albertine personifies the object of desire *en fuite*: all of Marcel's efforts aim at capturing her, yet the thought of possessing her is also frightening. Possession threatens to destroy her as the object of his desire; the Albertine who is desirable is the one who is beyond capture. Albertine's book, *La Prisonnière*, tells the story of Marcel's attempt at maintaining a relationship to his mistress best described as dynamic suspension: he must always hold himself between the fear of losing her and the danger of losing interest.

The structure of this suspension can be explored in a short passage, not untypical of *La Prisonnière* (III, 140-53). Marcel has just sent Albertine off to the Trocadéro, and in her absence, he is entertaining one of the shop girls he has had his eye on. His movements through the passage illustrate the constant attempt to maintain an equilibrium between the women, between distance and approach, and between separation and possession. Albertine's "anagramme enfantine" has convinced Marcel she is planning a secret rendezvous with Mlle Vinteuil at the Verdurins'—for he has not discovered that her story of friendship with the musician's lesbian daughter was a lie. To keep her from that suspected meeting, Marcel sends Albertine off to the Trocadéro Theater, certain that anything she could do there would be "forcément innocent." But since desire is a response to the frustrated project of possession, Marcel begins to lose interest once he is assured of control. There is, it seems to him, nothing Albertine could say which would surprise him; the woman possessed is a barrier to the imagination. He therefore shifts the direction of his desire, seeking the necessary "perpetual alliteration" in other women and other places. He does not yet realize that the text of her remarks, which represents his relationship to his mistress, will provide the void necessary to regenerate his interest.

The certainty that Albertine is safely confined brings boredom, and Marcel begins fantasizing about women not yet encountered with whom he can replace her. He recalls the image of a girl he has never met, but whom he remembers having glimpsed at the dairy. In the entire episode she is never identified more definitively than as "la crémière," yet another incarnation for Marcel of the conditions of desire: seen from afar, a face in a crowd, half-hidden and vague. In short, the circumstances in which Marcel discovered her describe the ideally desirable woman:

> Je ne l'avais vue que de loin, et en passant si vite que je n'aurais pu dire comment elle était. . . . D'ailleurs, le groupement autour d'elle de ses camarades n'avait pas été seul à m'empêcher de la bien voir, mais aussi l'incertitude des sentiments que je pouvais, à première vue et ensuite, lui inspirer. . . . (III, 139-40)

In his memory, Marcel sees her as a flash of blonde, recalled but faintly, perhaps even half-imagined. Despire this—or possibly because of it—the *crémière* becomes the figure offering the potential fulfillment of his fantasies. She is ideal, but Marcel must insist on her indisputable actuality as a dairymaid: "Elle n'était ni nue, ni déguisée, mais *une vraie crémière*" (III, 141). Like the imaginary peasant girl from Roussainville, she seems the image of his desires come to life. Most importantly, she combines in herself the real girl and the ideal desire she inspires: literally the incarnation of his fantasies in the "other," the real woman. Marcel wants to possess his ideal woman in the flesh, and the dairymaid seems to offer him the girl desired from a distance.

She must embrace him with the very same arms that carried her wares, "entourer notre cou de ces bras qui portaient les fruits," and return his desire with the same proud and unapproachable eyes that first defied and attracted him.

The glimpse of blonde in the distance is a center of minimal reality around which Marcel's fantasies can crystallize and allow his imagination to inscribe into his image of the girl the crucial distance of desire:

> Ces suppositions alternatives que j'avais faites en une seconde à son sujet, avaient épaissi autour d'elle l'atmosphère trouble où elle se dérobait, comme une déesse dans la nue que fait trembler la foudre. (III, 140)

The language recalls the elusive center of Albertine, which acted on him like an invisible deity. The *crémière* embodies Marcel's fantasies, just as the objects in Elstir's paintings assume a charm of their own when they express the artist's vision. Like the Duchesse de Guermantes, the *crémière* joins the mythic to the real world, evoking for Marcel the possibility of reaching the divine in real life:

> [E]lle était un peu de ce qui fait l'éternel désir, l'éternel regret de la vie, dont le double courant est enfin détourné, amené auprès de nous. Double, car s'il s'agit d'inconnu, d'un être deviné devoir être divin . . . on veut cette femme . . . nous permettant de nous évader dans ce monde. (III, 141-42)

She plays the same role for Marcel as Adrienne did for Gérard in Nerval's *Sylvie*. The project that attracted Proust's attention there was the attempt to reach the ideal world through its earthly manifestation. Gérard says of his era, "L'homme matériel aspirait au bouquet de roses qui devait le régénérer par les mains de la belle Isis."[5] The dairymaid represents the possibility, for Marcel, of the goddess coming into his room, offering the same juxtaposition of realities that aroused the "trouble inconnu" in Gérard when he touched Adrienne's hand. The force and scope of figural language will be seized through its literal element; the image will be possessed through its specific incarnation. As the *crémière* approaches, Marcel's excitement is heightened: this is no prostitute, he realizes, a woman who robs us of desire by offering herself before we have even tried to arouse her interest, nor an actress playing a role tailored to our demands, but "une vraie crémière," who *as she is*, and indisputably "other," nevertheless corresponds to the image of his desire. She will give him, he imagines, a privileged access to and possession of an imaginary ideal through her literal person, the impossible union of self and "other," imagination and world. She is the "être de fuite" come to his arms and offering him the possibility of physically possessing the woman seen from afar.

Marcel's main problem is what to expect when the crucial distance of desire is eliminated, when those girls approach "qu'on s'imagine si jolies quand on n'a pas le temps de s'approcher d'elles" (III, 141). He knows that once they are in his arms, "elles ne sont plus ce qu'elles étaient, cette distance que nous rêvions de franchir est supprimée" (III, 143). Indeed, as she comes closer and possession threatens to become an actuality, this living figment of Marcel's imagination is suddenly deflated and becomes *merely* a dairymaid. She is reduced to her own mere literality, no longer able to incarnate Marcel's vision of her. She can be possessed, that is, only in a particular form, in her proper materiality, which cannot fail to disappoint Marcel:

> Hélas! une fois auprès de moi, la blonde crémière aux mèches striées, dépouillée de tant d'imagination et de désirs éveillés en moi, se trouva réduite à elle-même. (III, 143)

Marcel has understood that

> Au reste, si l'on cherche à faire tenir dans une formule la loi de nos curiosités amoureuses, il faudrait la chercher dans le maximum d'écart entre une femme aperçue et une femme approchée, caressée. (III, 142)

The imagination and desire are stifled by the specificity and weight of the material object. Albertine eludes Marcel and maintains desire because her language is *mensonge*: even "decoded," her lies can defy and surprise him. His reading is invariably inadequate, never defining the lie, but merely noting its presence without overcoming the disjunction it opens up between fiction and knowledge. In this respect, Albertine resembles a person or object named in a work of fiction, always resisting the attempt to move towards her. Her language never defines an object, but only its absence. The *crémière*, by contrast, is the emblem of approach. If Albertine is like the dress in the story, the *crémière* is the Princesse's dress as it appears at a party: separated from its fictional context, its particularity eclipses the void opened by the fictional object. When the *crémière* approaches and becomes fully particularized, the "être de fuite" in her dies:

> Ce vol capturé, inerte, anéanti, incapable de rien ajouter à sa pauvre évidence, n'avait plus mon imagination pour collaborer avec lui. (III, 143)

Approach and possession cancel the crucial *écart* through which the imagination operates. The figural dimension and suggestiveness which the image broached have been crushed under what Marcel once called "l'écrasante pression de la matière" (III, 56).

What Marcel desired was not the "bird," but its flight. Once captured, it has lost that "vol," and the hunter is left with only the dead weight of her body. The flight ceases, and the girl is reduced to her simple self—an immobile and singular reality. However, Marcel's efforts do not end with this failure;

so long as his project is inspired by an illusion "sincerely" believed, failure is only a prelude to a new beginning:

> Mais on recommence avec d'autres femmes, on donne à ces entreprises tout son temps, tout son argent. . . . Ce premier rendez-vous, on sait pourtant qu'il accomplira l'évanouissement d'une illusion. Il n'importe: tant que l'illusion dure, on veut voir si on peut la changer en réalité. (III, 143)

Like Gérard, he must move toward the object of desire. In the words of Proust's essay on Nerval, "La passion croit son objet réel, l'amant de rêve d'un pays veut le voir. Sans cela, ce ne serait pas sincère" (*CSB*, pp. 241-42). The illusion of potential success is a necessary premise for the attempt at appropriation, and the episode of the dairymaid, in addition to being a story of failure, is also that of the regeneration of the illusion and repetition of the attempt. Marcel can begin again each time, because each manifestation of his fantasy is complete, denying the history of past failures and taking itself completely seriously. The conviction that success is possible *this time*, that this appearance of the ideal will allow itself to be realized, is an extension of Marcel's refusal to substitute one woman for another. The ability to invest the present incarnation of desire with the possibilities of the entire project of appropriation is what characterizes illusion as such. Conveying this impression is *how* the illusion is deceptive.

For Marcel, illusion refers to the conviction that he can possess in the flesh the very same woman who excited his desire from a distance, and that he, like Gérard, can "toucher du doigt mon idéal." It postulates the impossible identity of two levels of reality whereby the fictional (figural) essence would be seized through its expression in empirical (literal) reality. The project is analogous to Marcel's trip to Balbec, an attempt to make the name and the place coincide, or to Proust's indulgent hope that the train through Chantilly would take him to the landscape of *Sylvie*. As Proust pointed out in the Nerval essay, the sophisticate would have this troubled disjunction "par calcul," but one cannot save oneself the trouble of committing the error of literalism. The hope that the *crémière* would come to Marcel as the *same* girl he saw in the crowd is the same hope which inspired Gérard to return to the Valois in order to find his innocence incarnated in the *same* Sylvie he once knew. The illusion is founded on the particular, and unless Marcel gives it all his energy and belief, the illusion is not complete, which is to say it is not illusion at all but diversion. The possibility of success is so convincing that, like the artifice of the Princesse de Cadignan, it robs Marcel of the means to distinguish it as illusion. And like the woman born, "comme Eve naquit d'une côte d'Adam," during Marcel's sleep from his desire and "une fausse position de ma cuisse" (I, 4), the image Marcel creates embodies his fantasies so successfully as to hide the true source of their attraction—until the actual girl approaches close enough to shatter the illusion by becoming merely herself.

The incident with the *crémière* must be seen as part of an ongoing project, of which his experience with Albertine is a far more elaborate variation. As one image is destroyed, the project is renewed in other forms and other women: "la paysanne" of the Combray countryside, "la fillette" seen from Mme de Villeparisis's coach, or "la belle pêcheuse" near Balbec. None of them can hold his interest: the inevitable loss of desire necessitates an "alliteration" of desire. Only the most fundamentally elusive, or perhaps the most artful, woman can be "en fuite" even while in her lover's arms, at the moment of physical possession. Odette accomplished this for Swann, and Albertine similarly manages to avoid the fate of the *crémière* by always eluding Marcel and resisting certainty. If he is able to contain her in the present moment, the depth of her past and her intentions escape his control. Although he may possess her physically and capture her in his apartment, Marcel only enjoys what might be called a "horizontal possession" of his mistress. Thus, while the dairymaid must continually be replaced, Albertine is capable of rekindling Marcel's interest by regenerating the illusion that incites him. She eludes him as though distance and absence were an integral part of her image: she is capable of continually renewing her disappearance. Marcel complains that she is not a single person at all: she is a multiplication of herself—or a set of unconnected fragments, "Car je ne possédais dans ma mémoire que des séries d'Albertine séparées les unes des autres, incomplètes, des profils" (III, 149). Her image exhibits what Poulet called "un excès de richesse."[6] Rather than tending toward a unifying center, it explodes into its different aspects, into what Marcel once called "une multiplication d'elle-même" (III, 69). The *crémière* is highly specific, one particular manifestation of Marcel's desire; she is replaceable, but *la crémière* is incapable of herself becoming "many" *crémières*. Albertine, however, is an "allitération perpétuelle" for Marcel, constitutionally capable of becoming "many" Albertines. That lack of a center, that evasive multiplicity, is an integral part of Marcel's conception of her. She is, in a sense, the dairymaid who can multiply her image.

The figure of Albertine shares many qualities with a fictional text, defying approach and retaining always the ability to defeat the reader's expectations, changing its form, its direction, and its significance. On numerous occasions, Marcel discovers through Albertine what Proust learned from his experience with Ruskin and Nerval: that the pilgrimage to a fictional place or object is a necessary but erroneous project, destined to failure. The fictional image appears to offer an ideal in a particular object; approach only yields the physical object, while the image continues to elude the voyager.

> Les géographes, les archéologues nous conduisent bien dans l'île de Calypso, exhument bien le palais de Minos. Seulement Calypso n'est plus qu'une femme, Minos, qu'un roi sans rien de divin. (I, 949)

Proust has made clear in his early essays that this movement of approach is an error of reading and, actually, an evasion of the text. It is the idolatrous movement away from Ruskin and toward Venice, toward the convent in Holland, toward Illiers—as though the secret of the text were to be seized there. When geographers locate the exact island of Calypso, she ceases to be a poetic creation and becomes merely a woman of the same name. The *crémière* expresses the necessary *repetition* of Marcel's illusion, but Albertine, renewing her elusiveness like Diane de Cadignan, represents its persistence. These two forms of the theme of capture overlap ingeniously to create the crisis in *La Prisonnière* which prefigures Albertine's ultimate escape.

Once Albertine has been dispatched to the Trocadéro and the dairymaid enticed into his room (on the pretense of an errand), Marcel discovers that approach has made her unexciting and wants only to be rid of her. Yet he feels obliged to continue the ruse he employed to bring her there—an indication that his own fiction is beginning to master him, to exceed his intentions. He leafs through the *Figaro*, pretending to search for the object of his errand, and discovers by chance that Mlle Léa, a lesbian actress he has long suspected of having designs on Albertine, is appearing at the Trocadéro. This "coincidence" displays the characteristic Proustian mode of discovery in which, as Poulet has remarked, whatever secret he uncovers "n'est pas précisément celui qu'il voulait découvrir."[7] But reading itself has a pronounced tendency to exceed expectations; like Gérard's casual glance at the financial page in *Sylvie*, Marcel's reading of the *Figaro* takes him well beyond his original intentions. He recalls in panic the interest Léa and Albertine showed in each other at their first meeting in the Casino at Balbec, and in an instant, all Marcel's fears and suspicions have been redefined. They now have a new object and direction which completely disregards the previous object; there is no continuity: "Hier je craignais qu'Albertine n'allât chez Mme Verdurin. Maintenant je n'étais plus préoccupé que de Léa" (III, 151). In his "preoccupation," Marcel seizes one point of evidence and one interpretation to the exclusion of all other possible meanings. He is immobilized in his strategy by these minute details and locked into atomized moments of time. Now the only threat and object of his concern is Léa, but only yesterday, this threat was unimaginable, and the only conceivable danger was Mlle Vinteuil. What is most interesting is the way the one figure can replace the other. The Albertine that Marcel is trying to capture is a hydra: a new and more troubling threat to his control, a new image, arises to replace the one he has nearly circumscribed. Marcel remarks about a lover's doubt of his mistress's fidelity, "[A]rriverions-nous à le détruire, qu'il serait remplacé par un autre aussitôt" (III, 151). The multiplicity which continues to excite him continues also to defeat him. Léa and Mlle Vinteuil are manifestations of the same danger: lost control of Albertine; yet Marcel responds to each potential infidelity as though its prevention were the final and decisive link in the chain encompassing his mistress.

In his attempt to control Albertine, Marcel is caught between minute details which block his path and her total essence which eludes him:

> En ce moment, qu'[Albertine] ne retrouvât pas les deux jeunes filles et savoir si elle connaissait Léa ou non était ce qui me préoccupait le plus, bien qu'on ne dût pas s'intéresser aux faits particuliers autrement qu'à cause de leur signification générale, et malgré la puérilité qu'il y a, aussi grande que celle du voyage ou du désir de connaître des femmes, à fragmenter sa curiosité sur ce qui, du torrent invisible des réalités cruelles qui nous resteront toujours inconnues, a fortuitement cristallisé dans notre esprit. (III, 151)

Marcel responds to his dilemma with a twofold strategy, preventing the rendezvous with Léa ("qu'elle ne retrouvât pas") and learning definitively whether or not ("savoir si") Albertine has ever actually known the actress—a strategy corresponding to the disjunction he faces. In his preoccupation, Marcel is disturbed by the sense that no single detail will yield the "general significance" he seeks, for details invariably "fragment" his attention on facts which have crystallized only fortuitously out of the invisible torrent which is reality for him. Single moments are frozen and sacrifice precisely the flow he is chasing; they distract him from the whole.[8] But, of course, neither is there access to the whole "general significance" except through particular—albeit fortuitous—instances. The particular has a certain ineluctable reality to it; it cannot be foreseen. Marcel imagines he can anticipate surprise, but he is invariably astonished to discover *how* he is surprised:

> [L]e monde des possibles m'a toujours été plus ouvert que celui de la contingence réelle. Cela aide à connaître l'âme, mais on se laisse tromper par les individus. Ma jalousie naissait par des images, pour une souffrance, non d'après une probabilité. (III, 24)

Only the particular can make Marcel suffer,[9] but the particularities here cut him off from the whole. All that concerns him is the threat of this moment, even though he realizes that yesterday's obsession, now deemed harmless, was then just as vital and monolithic as today's. The image of Albertine with Léa has fully obliterated Mlle Vinteuil from Marcel's concern—just as his sudden anxiety over this new danger has blotted out the *crémière* still at his side. The interchangeability of Mlle Léa for earlier threats points up the futility of guaranteeing fidelity by hindering every possible encounter, or capturing the "être de fuite" by appropriating innumerable facts of her existence. This realization, however, in no way impedes his preoccupation; it produces, rather, the tension and syntactic confusion which characterize the entire passage.

The struggle to prevent Albertine's infidelities and the effort to find out all about her are precisely the tactics Marcel has used unsuccessfully throughout. When imprisonment failed to give him control, he sent friends out as spies and detectives. Andrée, Aimé, Bloch, and Saint-Loup have all been dispatched at one time or another to check on Albertine, collecting evidence that Marcel hopes will establish a center from which he can then judge his mistress with certainty. His attempt to seize her resembles an idolatrous reader's desire to grasp a text. She is an image he would capture by circumscribing it, assembling countless facts about her in order to comprehend the "text" by "cross-referencing" it. This is the same logic that inspired her physical imprisonment in his apartment, for he now trying to encircle and capture her past as he tried to confine her present. This investigation will also determine whether or not his fears are well-founded: by finding out the truth of her lesbian past, he can measure her potential for elusiveness in the future. But Albertine responds to his attempts like an irreducible rhetorical figure, an impossible juxtaposition of terms, a *non sequitur*. She is like her own text whose syntax Marcel describes as resembling an anacoluthon.

The way in which Marcel is distracted and misled by these preoccupations describes the activity of the reader of this passage. Like the narrator, his sense of the whole passage is impeded by an unavoidable preoccupation with its apparently disjunctive parts. "Fortuitement cristallisé" aptly describes the reader's attempt to make sense of this complex sentence. Marcel's afterthoughts and qualifications are intercalated into the syntactic complexity through which he takes us, while he tries to move away from the preoccupations of "ce moment." Confused by the long passage and difficult syntax, the reader assembles rather accidental groupings of meaning around the numerous subordinate clauses—*before* the whole sentence is apparent. Like a judge, he is continually being forced to determine significance before adequate evidence is at hand. Short pieces of meaning "fragment" his attention, causing it to crystallize "fortuitously" around the points which seem to offer a measure of syntactical clarity. The detail thus distracts and fragments attention, but also focuses it, even if fortuitously. Reading entails a set of *ad hoc* judgements that must continually be revised. In exchange for distraction and immobilization, the particular offers a temporarily stable constellation of meaning within which relationships become perceptible and measurable. The general significance Marcel is seeking only begins to emerge once he has committed himself to particular points and begun to establish a context. As Marcel well knows, the greater meaning often becomes apparent only long after the lover-judge has need for it. Details which come back to haunt him were ignored as insignificant at a time when he could have known them, and hidden facts which now seem so important were available "au temps où cela m'eût été indifférent" (III, 57). Albertine's language escapes him because the importance of her words is never clear until he has forgotten their significance.

Marcel's entire attempt is somewhat paradoxical inasmuch as he hopes to conquer the ethereal "être de fuite" with methods singularly concrete and particular. Leo Bersani has noticed this same paradox in Marcel's love affairs, remarking that "Marcel wants much more than physical possession, but physical possession is the short-cut to what he wants."[10] In fact, rather than being the "short-cut," physical possession is the detour Marcel knows he must take. The whole passage, and Marcel's strategy, revolve conspicuously around the qualification "bien qu'on ne dût pas," which holds in suspension the contradiction between the attempt and knowledge of its futility. Marcel is thus enacting syntactically precisely what he refuses to accept in Albertine: her ability to hold final significance "en suspens en elle." He sees—and acknowledges— the foolishness of his project, even while rushing toward details he hopes will capture the essence of his mistress. As with the girl seen from afar, "tant que l'illusion dure, on veut voir si on peut la changer en réalité." "Bien que . . ." is an admission not only of the project's inadequacy but also of its irresistibility; it verifies the "sincérité" of his endeavor. Ironically, probably no one can better appreciate the impossibility of controlling Albertine than Marcel. As the teller of Swann's story, he knows it to be the tale of Odette's elusiveness. But a woman can inspire desire that defies mere knowledge of past failures— by offering the illusory possibility of capture. When Marcel acknowledges that Albertine "était de ces femmes à qui leurs fautes pourraient au besoin tenir lieu de charme" (III, 150), he is not only referring to the sins which attract him but to the *constitutive void* at the heart, which is the original sin of the desired woman:

> Ce qui rend douloureuses de telles amours, en effet, c'est qu'il leur préexiste une espèce de péché originel de la femme, un péché qui nous les fait aimer. (III, 151)

Her secret attraction is that she seems to offer the final key to her elusiveness in whatever aspect she withholds.

Most of what we learn about Albertine is a function of Marcel's perceptions and attitudes, and similarly, for many of the characters in the *Recherche*, the change noticed in them is more a description of our changing impressions than of their own evolution: they are revealed through the novel rather than developed. Charlus, for example, is seen in numerous perspectives in the course of the story, each one of which describes the incompleteness or inadequacy of the previous image. This is likewise true for Morel, Saint-Loup, Gilberte, and many others. In the strategy of surprise, their images are more a function of our ignorance and of Marcel's, than of knowledge. Each new revelation or realization makes the old impression obsolete, demanding a fresh understanding of who this person is and, often, a complete redefinition of past evidence. Each image corresponds to a moment of comprehension in time, one that immobilizes all the evidence available into a meaningful configuration. Marcel's encounters with Charlus become a lesson in the need for constant revision, whereas the *crémière* who approaches the narrator freezes her many images into a single view. Her multiplicity, the demand for redefinition, falls victim to her insistent particularity, and like her physical features, her image is reduced to a stifling singularity:

> Hélas! une fois auprès de moi, la blonde crémière . . . [réduite à elle-même] prenait un air tout penaud de n'avoir plus (au lieu des dix, des vingt, que je me rappelais tour à tour sans pouvoir fixer mon souvenir) qu'un seul nez . . . [qui] avait en tout cas perdu le pouvoir de se multiplier. (III, 143)

The girl at a distance offers too many possibilities and must continually be reread, but approach marks the end of reading, reducing suggestion to certainty and figural language to its literal minimum. Like a fictional text itself, Albertine is a character who can focus the need for rereading into every instant, for she is always exploding into uncontrollable multiplicity. As Poulet perceived, "Albertine décuplée, multipliée, c'est déjà Albertine disparue."[11] She personifies the elusive image, always defying a single reading, and forever in the act of disappearing. She always offers Marcel the possibility of success, but withholds certainty. As Swann found out from Odette, Marcel learns that mastery is defeated not by superior force, but by doubt. Albertine becomes a unified figure—but only a hypothetical one—through Marcel's desire, for when a lover talks about the woman he desires, Marcel realizes, "[L]a stabilité de nature que nous lui prêtons n'est que fictive et pour la commodité du langage" (III, 64-65). She is only constituted as a whole through memory, when she herself is absent. Albertine creates—and perhaps she is herself—the illusion of realizing one's fantasy, and she holds Marcel between the worlds of "reality" and "fantasy" as the girl Sylvie did for Gérard or the story *Sylvie* did for Proust.

It is hardly accidental, then, that in describing the "puerility" of his attempt, Marcel evokes two central Proustian motifs which "fragment" the imagination: *le voyage* and *le désir de connaître des femmes*. As in the attempt to seize Balbec through Albertine, both themes express the tantalizing possibility of capturing the image of one's fantasy. Marcel has remarked just previously that "La curiosité amoureuse est comme celle qu'excitent en nous les noms de pays: toujours déçue, elle renaît et reste toujours insatiable" (III, 143). Like the names of countries or the names of the nobility, the image of the woman desired seems to incarnate the imagination into a real form, and thus to belong to both worlds. By offering the apparently real possibility of voyaging from the real to the fictional world, the image becomes the source of the *trouble* Proust knows when his train passes through the towns Nerval named: he feels suddenly that for once he *can* indulge his desire and reach the essence of *Sylvie* through the geographical reality.

The failure to capture Albertine has been prefigured in Marcel's earlier frustration with the apparently accidental quality of his loves. "True love," for Marcel, must be totally specific in order to verify the presence of the "other." He despairs of finding a language specific enough to address itself exclusively to the woman he loves. The terms of endearment he knows are all *formulas* of sentiment, applicable to any woman, and even his feelings, he complains, "ne sont pas en rapport étroit et nécessaire avec la femme aimée, mais passent à côté d'elle" (II, 829). His language, like his love, cannot be sufficiently particular: "[L]e langage que nous lui avons tenu n'a pas été formé expressément pour elle, qu'il nous a servi, nous servira pour d'autres" (II, 829). While he was forgetting Gilberte, Marcel berated himself for the cheapness of his sentiments and their distance from true love, for he could already feel he would soon be able to direct the love he had felt for Gilberte toward another girl:

> [O]n est toujours détaché des êtres: quand on aime, on sent que cet amour ne porte pas leur nom, pourra dans l'avenir renaître, aurait même pu, dans le passé, naître, pour une autre et non pour celle-là. (I, 611)

The continuity he seeks in Albertine, he disparages in himself, probably because it exposes the subjectivity of his love, as well as that of Albertine's image. Through a fictional device of his own, Marcel begins to explore the manipulation of continuity in Albertine's language.

To coax her back from the theater before she can meet Mlle Léa, Marcel writes Albertine a note. Instead of confessing his jealousy, he claims to have received a letter from a woman (not Albertine) with whom he is very much in love. The letter has made him very sad, and he is in great need of Albertine's consolation. Only through this fiction can he ask her to return to him, but through his own fiction, he seems to discover how she eludes him. His suspicion and her lesbianism, he finds, are born of the same void: her elusiveness is already her infidelity. But whereas "spontaneous" lies are betrayed by their incompleteness and unmasked by new evidence or internal contradictions, the total lie enjoys a kind of impermeability. Albertine slips through Marcel's net by creating a fiction, an image of herself. She may offer contradictions "aussi décisives qu'un flagrant délit," yet when he is sure he has caught her, she introduces a radical discontinuity into her confession—into which she disappears:

> [P]rise en fraude comme un enfant, grâce à ce brusque redressement stratégique, Albertine avait chaque fois rendu vaines mes cruelles attaques et rétabli la situation. Cruelles pour moi. Elle usait, non par raffinement de style, mais pour réparer ses imprudences, de ces brusques sautes de syntaxe ressemblant un peu à ce que les grammairiens appellent anacoluthe ou je ne sais comment. (III, 152-53)

Too much denial betrays where truth lies, but a total lie, a total evasion, leaves no traces of its origin and is fully effective. Albertine's language defeats Marcel's interrogation because in the face of his hypothetical causality she manages to dissociate the incriminatory predicate from the apparent subject of the sentence:

> S'étant laissée aller, en parlant femmes, à dire: "Je me rappelle que dernièrement je," brusquement, après un "quart de soupir," "je" devenait "elle." (III, 153)

Albertine's anacoluthon has ruptured the continuity necessary to link the evidence to the culprit. "Anacoluthe" is defined by Robert as "absence de suite," but it is also an absence of origin here. In Albertine's *dédoublement*, the original subject is lost and replaced by a fictional subject: the *moi* which began the incriminatory sentence disappears into the syntactic gulf between the beginning of the statement and its conclusion, while the fictional *moi*, Albertine's "elle," assumes the role of the guilty party. The discontinuity between the roles not only frees Albertine from her involuntary accusation, but proves her innocence by separating her from the real malefactor. A symmetry between Marcel's and Albertine's roles emerges which marks the latter as a writer. Marcel is clearly a reader of evidence, attempting, like a judge, to penetrate the center from which the facts seem to emanate. But the writer, like Albertine, postulates a fictional center around which the evidence then appears to accumulate as a causal result. Whereas Marcel, in his search, is trying to seize his self (his fantasies and ideals) in the "other," Albertine disappears into that "other." Her fiction is able to liberate itself from real causality; it has no sufficient cause. Albertine does not hide in the midst of her revelation, but turns away, emptying the evidence of its capacity to incriminate *her*; its *sens* is changed:

> [C]'était une chose qu'elle avait aperçue en promeneuse innocente, et nullement accomplie. Ce n'était pas elle qui était le sujet de l'action. (III, 153)

Simple lies, Marcel discovers, are a mask of reality, a departure from it, and taking their origin in truth, they can be betrayed by it. But the force of fiction lies in its ability to conceal the separation of subjects. It is an untraceable leap from reality, relating to it only as one part of an anacoluthon to the other—that is, without connection. Albertine's device here, her strategy of evasion, is no mere stylistic cosmetic. It involves a radical leap into fiction: the sudden creation of a world entire and logical, and complete with past and present. As Marcel will rediscover encountering Mme Verdurin at the final party of the novel, this device creates its own history at the moment it comes into being. This is neither an approximation to truth nor "un mensonge improvisé." Albertine is not in fact just using this device, she is turning herself into it. The clear evidence, violently detached from the speaker, is vitiated and becomes a mere story. The narrative creation of a "third person" exculpates the narrator: Albertine is no longer the subject of the perversions she describes but, like

Marcel himself, only a spectator and therefore "forcément innocente." Once again Marcel discovers, as Swann did, that the void which the woman offers and which defeats his approach is what is most attractive in her. The original sin that he has inscribed into her image is an original lack.

The Albertine that Marcel is chasing disappears into a fictional being about whom everything must be learned from inside the story, but who does not exist outside her narrative. The girl telling the story separates herself totally from the character "elle"; Albertine has become another "moi." The empirical Albertine steps aside, leaving Marcel to uncover facts applicable only to "elle." He finds himself pursuing a figure with no meaningful connection to the girl he desires. Like Sainte-Beuve attempting to seize the essence of a work through details of the author's life, Marcel is engaged in a mistaken search for origins, chasing the wrong *moi* and trying to surprise the text through biographical and moral research. We are reminded of Proust's famous warning to Gide, "Vous pouvez tout raconter, mais à condition de ne jamais dire 'je.' "[12]

Marcel's investigation is most decisively defeated by Albertine's ability to cover the traces of her leap by assuming a complete past at the very moment of the image's inception. The fictional "elle" insists upon, and defines herself through, this instant history. The power of her fiction lies in reflecting its existence back into the time before the leap. Once Albertine "becomes" a spectator, she has always been one—and "elle" has always already been the subject of Albertine's narrative. Marcel's attempt to seize Albertine at the origin of her text, at the point where she first begins to escape into fiction, is thus doomed to failure. Since the text has always been fictional and its subject always "other," he must always begin again:

> J'aurais voulu me rappeler exactement le commencement de la phrase pour conclure moi-même, puisqu'elle lâchait pied, à ce qu'en eût été la fin. Mais comme j'avais attendu cette fin, je me rappelais mal le commencement. (III, 153)

This necessity to reread, to begin again, is of course characteristic of the *Recherche* as a whole. This is a book built around surprises, as every character reappears bringing new revelations which demand that the reader, along with Marcel, redefine his understanding. If the novel is seen as progressing toward a clear achievement, it must be determined how, if at all, this need to begin again ceases or is transcended.

The development of the characters of the *Recherche* seems to "wind up" somewhere, but how is this sense of knowing them that we have toward the end of the work essentially different from the deceptive impressions we had earlier? Charlus, and even Saint-Loup, seem to end, finally, as homosexuals. Andrée, of course, but also Mme Verdurin, Odette, and even Gilberte may finally be lesbians. Yet it would be a serious mistake to see this "culmination" as a final, which is to say a *truthful*, identification. Homosexuality is the epitome, rather than the end point, of metamorphosis. It is the mask *par excellence*, just as Albertine's lesbianism is the height of elusiveness.[13] Morel, furthermore, proves to Charlus that his bisexuality is emblematic of the reader's need constantly to redefine the text. When he discovers by chance an unmistakably frank letter to Morel from Léa, the actress renowned for her strictly female sexual preferences, the Baron is overwhelmed by the morass of imaginable relations between the lesbian and the bisexual Morel. The letter makes it clear that Léa is sexually interested in the Baron's violinist friend and seems to know all about his affairs with several of her lesbian friends, but Charlus is particularly disturbed by one remark addressed to Morel: "Toi, tu en es au moins" (III, 215). Now "en être" has always been an important expression for the exclusive Charlus; it has always meant being homosexual. In Léa's letter, however, it apparently refers to Morel's attraction for lesbian women. On the one hand, this shift excludes Charlus completely from the world of Morel and Léa, since the Baron cannot locate a role to play in this complex parody of heterosexuality where lesbian women desire homosexual men acting the parts of women. Yet more profoundly, this phrase troubles him because "en être" represents an entire act of self-recognition for Charlus. As a young man, Marcel tells us, he had had to discover through long experience that his tastes were not for women, and that in the code of the homophile, he was "one of those": "Après l'avoir d'abord ignoré, il avait enfin, depuis un temps bien long déjà, appris que lui-même 'en était' " (III, 215). Suddenly now, in confusion over the possible interest Léa could have in Morel, the Baron's firm understanding of himself and his language is shattered:

> Ainsi les êtres qui "en étaient" n'étaient pas seulement ceux qu'il avait crus, mais toute une immense partie de la planète . . . et le baron, devant la signification nouvelle d'un mot qui lui était si familier, se sentait torturé par une inquiétude de l'intelligence autant que du cœur, devant ce double mystère, où il y avait à la fois de l'agrandissement de sa jalousie et de l'insuffisance soudaine d'une définition. (III, 215)

The entire sense of "en être" has been "remis en question" for Charlus, and with it the unimpeachable conviction it represented: the finality of complete understanding—of himself, of language, of his world. The code that he had known so surely has proven itself inadequate; the situation demands a new constellation of meaning. His old definition—and with it perhaps all possibility of definitiveness—has failed him. His lesson in reading is the loss of all fixed definitions: the mask of language can assume *any* meaning.

What is true for language is also true for the characters of the novel. One critic, Howard Moss, seems quite right in refusing to admit equally all the permutations Proust introduces in his characters. The dissatisfaction he feels with respect to Saint-Loup's eventual homosexuality frees "the geometric progression of misconception" from its chronology in the novel. We are ultimately able to choose the aspects of a character which determine him for us, regardless of when they appear:

> Understanding Proust's ultimate argument, we do not quite accede to it. Marcel's original impressions of Saint-Loup and the Duchesse de Guermantes are more lasting than their decline into vice and banality.[14]

The lesson of continuous redefinition is often linked to the characters of ambiguous sexuality—but quite beyond the realm of mere sexuality. "Miss Sacripant" evokes a dialectic of identification by appearing to be at once an effeminate boy and a girl dressed as a man. In this respect she is part of Elstir's overall metaphorization of reality, like the land and sea which exchange their terms of description in his painting of the "Port de Carquethuit." And Léa, the same actress who writes to Morel, is also the source of a lesson in reading for Marcel—before the Trocadéro, at Balbec.

Already during the visit to Balbec, the narrator is disturbed by the interest Léa shows in Albertine. From the moment she enters the Casino where Marcel and Albertine are talking, he watches his mistress's reaction to the lesbian's attention. After a while, however, he reassures himself of her lack of interest, noticing that Albertine ignores Léa, even to the point of keeping her back turned to the actress's admiring stare. Only when Albertine shows Marcel the mirror behind him in which she has been following Léa's attentions with great interest does he appreciate how misguided his confidence was. His first "reading" of the situation is now seen to be grossly inadequate—not in its content, but in its configuration of the evidence, in its interpretation. The failure to capture Albertine is the failure to find a single, definitive reading of the evidence she presents. In this sense, she *is* the elusive fictional text itself. When his attention is drawn to the mirror, Albertine's turned back becomes a confirmation of guilt, rather than an exoneration. The first reading now appears to have been an inversion of the truth, its mirror-image, so to speak.

Marcel has to read the beginning and end of Albertine's sentences simultaneously in order to determine what direction to take. He must always be rereading, but his suspicion gives him no point at which to *start*. Faced with the lie at the end of her sentence, where "je" turns into "elle," Marcel imagines he must retrieve the truth which surely lay at the sentence's beginning, in that hypothetical lost past when judgement was still possible. Still, fiction's transparency defies the attempt to penetrate to the source from which Albertine's image seems to emanate. To capture that center, he would have to immobilize the image, destroying its desirable elusiveness:

> Et, en elles-mêmes, qu'étaient Albertine et Andrée? Pour le savoir, il faudrait vous immobiliser, . . . il faudrait ne plus vous aimer pour vous fixer. (III, 64)

Like the *fraîcheur* he felt along the Vivonne, the image of Albertine would be either lost or traced by the lover back to a fixed origin. The lover attempts to follow the text to its real, original intention, but the suggestiveness of the text, the possible meanings he can attach to the evidence, everywhere exceed his expectations and overwhelm the attempt to circumscribe them. The loss of Albertine, which must be seen as occurring at every point of their relationship, is the failure of Marcel's reading. It is the failure of the attempt at a comprehensive reading.

Marcel fails for the very same reasons that Albertine cannot prove her innocence in the face of suspicion:

> [Ces souvenirs] étaient comme un aveu total des goûts d'Albertine, une confession générale de son infidélité, contre quoi ne pouvaient prévaloir les serments particuliers d'Albertine. (III, 150)

Her particular denials simply cannot cope with all the implications which his suspicions can conjure up from her very protestations of innocence. These become merely further proof of her guilt. The essence "behind" her evidence escapes Marcel because he cannot determine which indications to follow. The lie is itself like the woman loved for her flaws, showing the lover only *that* she is gone—but not where:

> [L]es menteurs sont rarement pris, et parmi les menteurs, plus particulièrement les femmes qu'on aime. On ignore où elle est allée. . . . [L]e mensonge est perçu instantanément, et la jalousie redoublée, puisqu'on sent le mensonge et qu'on n'arrive pas à savoir la vérité. (III, 178)

The lie never allows itself to be reduced to simple "truth," nor the mask to simple identity. Jealousy is finally the sense of insufficiency at the text's response to interrogation. The evidence reveals either too little or too much, and jealousy is the feeling of having been cheated or fooled—to which the text responds with further deception:

> Dès que la jalousie est découverte, elle est considérée par celle qui en est l'objet comme une défiance qui autorise la tromperie. (III, 61)

The explosion of Albertine into many fragments makes each inadequate for Marcel. In his estimation, whatever image can be captured is *ipso facto* merely accidental and "fortuitement cristallisée," like the detailed impressions he once gathered (and rejected) along the *côté de Guermantes*. The reports about Albertine invariably raise more questions than they solve, and since they never take him back to her essence, poor Marcel is caught in an eternal search for beginnings—of her sentences, her lies, her experience:

Il en est malheureusement des commencements d'un mensonge de notre maîtresse comme des commencements de notre propre amour, ou d'une vocation. Ils se forment . . . passent inaperçus de notre propre attention. Quand on veut se rappeler de quelle façon on a commencé d'aimer une femme, on aime déjà. (III, 153)

As a reader, Marcel is attempting to seize Albertine's secret through her text. But when the text eludes him, like Sainte-Beuve he tries to reach its essence by locating its "original moment" outside the text, a sign which can supplement the inadequacy of the text itself.

5

Marcel's Fictional Project:
A Strategy of Recovery

Marcel's search for origins in his pursuit of Albertine is only part of his more general quest for a center, a reference point on which to base a clear and certain judgement. This search for the grounds of authenticity persists throughout the novel and comes to characterize his attempt to progress toward full understanding of his world. It motivates the sense of completeness of his work that we find in the final book, the tone of having achieved his vocational and artistic aims, like the "portraits" which are completed at the final party, "le Temps l'avait enfin poussée jusqu'à la plus parfaite ressemblance" (III, 936). The hunt for the "real" Guermantes, for the "essence" behind the trees at Hudimesnil, and for the "true" identity of Charlus share in this search for the genuine. For Marcel, the success of these ventures would mean going beyond mere detail and seeing clearly enough to judge. Success implies reaching beyond the particulars to a true essence and, in effect, redeeming lost time. Marcel portrays his movement through the novel as culminating in a reversal which corrects the distortions which have hampered clear perception. A crucial question, however, is whether the completeness and the kind of "correction" he asserts at the end are acceptable in the context of the novel as a whole.

The preceding discussion has shown that the possibility of clear judgement in the *Recherche*, for both reader and narrator, is repeatedly and deliberately challenged by the complexity of Marcel's world and the essential multivalence of language. In light of these difficulties, Marcel's progress toward clarity of perception, implicit in the achievement of his vocation and in the claim to self-transparency typical of *Le Temps retrouvé*, must be reexamined in the context of his entire search for authenticity. By following that search, seen in Marcel's changing views of the role played by the nobility, a central emblem of the genuine for him, it may be possible to discern a movement running counter to Marcel's triumphant conclusion. It must always be remembered that part of the narrator's desire in telling his story is to have his novel read as a *successful* odyssey. As Leo Bersani has noted,

[Marcel] deliberately organizes the story of his life so that we may see it as he himself has come to see it: as the story of his "invisible vocation."[1]

In the elusiveness of judgement, we discovered the endless need to redefine one's world in order to make sense out of it. Albertine further demonstrated the impossibility of appropriating the "other" and of seizing the essence of a text directly. But in the last book, it is the disintegration of the aristocracy which is played against the apparent achievement of Marcel's goals. The steadily declining value of the nobility precisely—but inversely—reflects Marcel's progress toward his vocation. An examination of the role of the nobility, seen as Marcel's paradigm of the sacred and as the principle of the authentic, will show how countercurrents in the narrative serve to complicate and redirect the significance of the narrator's linear progress.

René Girard has observed that the Proustian world is marked not so much by the absence of the sacred as by its profanation,[2] yet for Marcel, the "sacred" is that which can authenticate his efforts.[3] In his eyes, the members of the nobility have always enjoyed a privileged access to the authentic: in their names they seemed to contain both history and place, making them the point at which the various errors of idolatry converge. Through this link, and through the Guermantes, the aristocrats are also associated with his attempt to find his vocation. In this respect, his pursuit of Mme de Guermantes is like his quest for the essence of Albertine: each detail shows itself only an accidental manifestation of the genuine. No longer self-evident, the essence of the genuine must be *made* apparent, as Marcel imagines it was before particularization obscured it. In his art, Marcel is searching for a counterpart to his early vision of the Duchesse, for a language which is purely figural and free of the mere accidents of form. The image of Mme de Guermantes transcends its particularity, for she incarnates the line of the Guermantes, the chosen race of Combray. It is in her eyes that Marcel most keenly feels the regret of not being a writer: the *côté de Guermantes* is the place where he feels that he *should* be an artist:

[J]'étais ramené par le flot sonore [de la Sonate] vers les jours de Combray—je ne veux pas dire de Montjouvain et du côté de Méséglise, mais des promenades du côté de Guermantes—où j'avais désiré d'être un artiste. (III, 158)

Here along the banks of the Vivonne, where he decided to return "avec des lignes," is where he sensed that his vocation lay away from the fine observations and preoccupation with detail, the "special pleasures" which distract and fascinate him. Details seem a waste of time, for they never lead him to the transcendent vision "behind," as the nobility promises to do. But ultimately, the way in which the aristocracy fails Marcel as the model point of reference, and fails even its own principles, will show how a certain failure of language is inevitable and is even inscribed in the structure of the *Recherche*. We should not forget that the moment when Marcel seems at last to have seized his vision and his vocation is also the instant he confronts, in cataclysmic form, the final downfall of the nobility. At the last party of the novel, Marcel discovers that the Princesse de Guermantes, who has always represented the purest and noblest qualities of the aristocracy, has been supplanted in name and station by the vulgar and bourgeois Mme Verdurin. Marcel's discovery of his vocation must therefore be examined in the context of the fate of the nobility with which it has been so closely associated.

Marcel's discovery at the final party portends more than simply the breakdown of a social code. The aristocracy has functioned for him as a principle of exclusivity, the distinction which can never be earned, and thus an inimitable and irreplaceable social order. As an irrefutable center, the aristocracy offers an absolute measure of moral value and guarantees society contact with a source of genuine quality, historically verifiable. It based its claim on a clear genealogical contiguity to an origin, its purity protected for centuries by careful inbreeding. Since a person is either born noble or he is not, his title is his history, and his claim an open book: the Gotha. A commoner can no more hope to become noble than he can expect to redraw the lines of his ancestry, and this is what assures the aristocratic guarantee of value. As Charlus tells M. de Cambremer in his haughty lesson in protocol, "Mais que voulez-vous, l'histoire est l'histoire, nous n'y pouvons rien et il ne dépend pas de nous de la refaire" (II, 946-47). The aristocratic grounds of social difference assure value by their irrefutable link to place and to the past. The noble name marks an historical descent from a nearly mythical moment in the past, a vision embodied for Marcel in the Duchesse de Guermantes. Her ancestry, going back to Geneviève de Brabant, the figure in the magic lantern, touches a lost point in the past, yet she is herself undeniably real. Like the Roussainville peasant girl, she joins the genius of the region to herself, for through her name and race she is a part of the countryside Marcel sees and of the landscape of his vocation:

> Jamais dans la promenade du côté de Guermantes nous ne pûmes remonter jusqu'aux sources de la Vivonne. . . . Jamais non plus nous ne pûmes pousser jusqu'au terme que j'eusse tant souhaité d'atteindre, jusqu'à Guermantes. Je savais que là résidaient des châtelains, le duc et la duchesse de Guermantes, je savais qu'ils étaient des personnages réels et acutellement existants, mais chaque fois que je pensais à eux, je me les représentais tantôt en tapisserie, comme était la comtesse de Guermantes dans le "Couronnement d'Esther" de notre église, tantôt de nuances changeantes, comme était Gilbert le Mauvais dans le vitrail . . . tantôt tout à fait impalpables comme l'image de Geneviève de Brabant, ancêtre de la famille de Guermantes . . . (I, 171)

The special role of the Duchesse for Marcel derives from the fact that she is in contact with the mythic in his world—yet she is indisputably real. The search for the real Duchesse, that incarnation of true nobility, is like the search for the unimaginable source of the Vivonne, and like that origin, the Duchesse is able to postpone almost indefinitely the moment of being reached. Her image remains at an insuperable distance from young Marcel; one even finds that he struggles to maintain that distance and the image it preserves.

The Duchesse stands alongside the mythical Geneviève de Brabant, sharing the religious aura of her ancestors in the stained-glass windows of Saint-Hilaire, but like the woman seen from afar, she incarnates the ideal image in the real world. As only the nobility can, the Duc and the Duchesse embody the name and the land; they *are* Combray, the territory of Guermantes, its feudal masters whose presence is in the region and who therefore need not actually live there. With a past "presque descendu dans la terre" (I, 167), they partake of the land in a manner peculiar to the aristocracy, creating in Marcel the conviction that something essential, participating somehow in that mythic origin and independent of any single Guermantes, is transmitted from one generation to another. Yet in the course of the novel, the nobility inexorably loses that special quality and its promise for Marcel, and one important aspect of the *Recherche* is the story of that loss. For the remainder of the discussion, we will focus on the nature and implications of that loss as a deliberate countercurrent to Marcel's progress. It is not by chance that the guarantor of authenticity and plenitude is undermined at the moment Marcel seems to assert the wholeness of his vision.

As Marcel becomes increasingly familiar with the Guermantes, their magic diminishes, obscured by their inescapable concreteness and individuality. When his family moves in adjacent to the Hôtel de Guermantes, the Duchesse, now all too visible, starts to lose the spiritual dimension she offered Marcel. He describes the process in images of weight, as though her ethereality could not bear the burden of her substance. She has become "comme un cygne ou un saule en lequel a été changé un dieu ou une nymphe et qui désormais, [est] soumis aux lois de la nature" (II, 29). After years of social contact, Marcel will again describe her as a figure which has lost its ability to transform itself.

> [U]ne dame qui n'était déjà plus pour moi qu'une dame comme une autre, et qui m'avait quelquefois invité, non à descendre dans le royaume sous-marin des Néréides, mais à passer la soirée dans la baignoire de sa cousine. (III, 1008)

Her image has lost its figural power, reducing the Duchesse to her literal self. At each stage of his entrance into society, it seems, Marcel will reenact this drama of disappointment. And although the gatherings he attends follow an ascending social register, their increased height inevitably is accompanied by a diminished notion of how important and exhilarating that height is. Seen close up, the vision of the Duchesse is sullied by the superficiality of her famous wit and by her callousness; the famous Guermantes genealogy becomes obscured by the tedious incantations of lineage that fill the conversation of Charlus or the Prince de Guermantes. The more familiar Marcel becomes with the Faubourg, the less impressive become the noble figures inhabiting it.

At first, Marcel is able to overcome his disappointment and preserve his ideal by redefining his perceptions or by placing the true aura at a further remove, "replacing" the Duchesse, as Michel Butor remarked, with the even more mythical figure of the Princesse de Guermantes, "toute blancheur et mythologie."[4] But it is essential to appreciate that the nobility is suffering its own decline, apart from, yet parallel to, Marcel's experience of approach.[5] By the time of the final party, the Duchesse has virtually abdicated her position in the Faubourg for the company of the actress Rachel and other artists. Charlus, another exemplary figure of the nobility, has reached such degradation that Marcel feels compelled to describe to Bloch the death of the society of his youth by taking the Baron as a symbol of that world: "Swann est mort et M. de Charlus ne vaut guère mieux" (III, 954). In addition, cataclysmic political events have intervened on the social scene, with far-reaching consequences: the Dreyfus Affair and the First World War have dissolved many of the once absolute barriers between classes. And in the chaos of the "reclassement national," many bourgeois were able to use their politics to carve out a position in the previously impenetrable ranks of the aristocracy, for the exigencies of conflict threw together gentry and commoners of the same camp. Odette was naturally one of the more astute social manipulators.

> Mme Swann avait gagné à cette attitude d'entrer dans quelques-unes des ligues de femmes du monde antisémites qui commençaient à se former et avait noué des relations avec plusieurs personnes de l'aristocratie. (II, 253)

This decline has been perceptible through the entire novel, but at the party of the Princesse, at the end, Marcel suddenly seems to confront the sum total of this evolution.

The scene strikes Marcel as a "coup de théâtre," for he has been away so long that even the figures he recognizes seem to be in disguise, yet the transformation he notices is far more profound than the ravages of time on the faces of his old friends. He is shocked to find untutored newcomers joining the social climbers Bloch and Legrandin in the salon where the Prince of Wales once walked comfortably among his peers. This is an infernal masquerade, a far cry from the costume the Duchesse wore, around which Marcel's first vision crystallized. Even Odette's costume as "Miss Sacripant" carries only faint overtones of perversion, but the disguise at the Princesse's party is far more insidious, both the means and the symbol of the fall of the nobility. The party itself seems a travesty of Marcel's earlier visits to the Faubourg and of the values it once represented.

Marcel is stunned by the impure mixture: the bourgeois snobs of his youth are accepted now as familiar faces amid the highest nobility. The aristocracy seems to have lowered itself to the level of the climbers Bloch and Legrandin, yet what disturbs him most is that no one is aware of the change. For some, the degradation of the nobility has been so gradual, like the work of time, that they have not noticed it. The others, the newcomers, have no memory and, consequently, no notion of value. They naturally accept the hierarchy of the present "comme si le passé n'existait pas":

> Les dîners, les fêtes mondaines, étaient pour l'Américaine une sorte d'Ecole Berlitz. Elle entendait les noms et les répétait sans avoir connu préalablement leur valeur, leur portée exacte. (III, 960)

The wealthy American visitors, for whom these parties are a "Berlitz School" of social graces, cannot judge the value of these figures, and since they have no experience or knowledge of the past, they cannot realize that "M. de Charlus avait eu la plus grande situation de Paris à une époque où Bloch n'en avait aucune" (III, 964). For the social novices, the society they see in the salon represents the eternal pinnacle of Parisian society. Its devaluation is beyond their comprehension, for they have lost the sense of history which gave meaning to those values.

New elements have been assimilated into high society, and new aristocrats have replaced the old, as sons will assume the titles of their fathers, but there is one important difference here of which Bloch has an intuition when Marcel presents him to the hostess:

> "[L]a maîtresse de maison d'ici, la princesse de Guermantes . . . Certes, je reconnais qu'elle a grand air, et elle a bien ces yeux extraordinaires dont tu me parlais, mais enfin je ne la trouve pas tellement inouïe que tu disais. Evidemment elle est très racée, mais enfin . . ."

Bloch has clearly noticed a certain disparity of quality, but only the narrator's memory can solve the puzzle of what is missing here:

> Je fus obligé de dire à Bloch qu'il ne me parlait pas de la même personne. La princesse de Guermantes en effet était morte, et c'est l'ex-madame Verdurin que le prince, ruiné par la défaite allemande, avait épousée. (III, 954-55)

This is of course also startling for the reader, and the narrator embellishes the discovery to bring out its full significance. Bloch remains skeptical of Marcel's explanation, since he possesses proof to the contrary: he has checked the Princesse's credentials in the Gotha, the public record of the nobility, and found her to be "tout ce qu'il y a de plus grandiose." This documentation is in fact what lies at the base of Marcel's shock: from the social game of "le bal travesti," the disguise has evolved into a subversion of the entire social structure. Those without memory and newcomers to the world of the Guermantes will never be able to discover the loss of essential values, because the theft has disguised itself so effectively as to efface all evidence of the loss.

Mme Verdurin, that relentless social politician and leader of her self-proclaimed exclusive clan, has taken the place of the woman who was the paragon of the Faubourg and who, for Marcel, embodied and preserved the ultimate vision of the nobility. Through a series of strategic marriages, Mme Verdurin has climbed the ladder of social standing. These marriages, in addition to being the means of penetrating the Faubourg, have enabled her to obliterate the evidence of her climb:

> En effet, Mme Verdurin, peu après la mort de son mari, avait épousé le vieux duc de Duras, ruiné, qui l'avait faite cousine du prince de Guermantes, et était mort après deux ans de mariage. Il avait été pour Mme Verdurin une transition fort utile, et maintenant celle-ci, par un troisième mariage, était princesse de Guermantes. (III, 955)

When Bloch checks her genealogy, he only learns that the Prince de Guermantes married the Duchesse de Duras. Her political skill has permitted her to recreate her past in the image of her present, substantiating her station, as it were, retroactively. Her position and genealogy both bear witness to the claim that she has *always* been of the highest aristocracy. By thus replacing ancestry with social success, Mme Verdurin has managed to call into question the nobility's entire assurance of authenticity.

Mme Verdurin's success undermines Marcel's principle of authenticity through her ability to obliterate all traces of its history. She not only uses a text—the Gotha—to authenticate her claim, but like Albertine, her whole strategy is essentially textual in nature. Fiction escapes the demands of reality by creating a past which can adequately and unimpeachably "account" for the present. The aristocracy preserved values that ordered society by guaranteeing an origin certified by history, but Mme Verdurin *duplicates* the credentials founded on uniqueness: she violates their irreplaceability. The flawless descent of the Princesse de Guermantes is counterfeited by Mme Verdurin's ambitious climb, an inversion of direction which marks the profanation of all that was most sacred in the nobility, for Marcel, and the force of its guarantee:

> Pour moi, dans cette identité de titre, de nom, qui faisait qu'il y avait encore une princesse de Guermantes et qu'elle n'avait *aucun rapport* [italics added] avec celle qui m'avait tant charmé et qui n'était plus là et qui était comme une morte sans défense à qui on l'eût volé, il y avait quelque chose [de douloureux]. (III, 955)

In addition to usurping the place of a woman with whom she has "no connection," Mme Verdurin is corrupting the identity which assured the nobility's integrity. Success masquerading as proper succession makes Marcel feel he is witnessing the perversion of a fundamental principle of authenticity. Where the Princesse stood as an absolute standard of value, Mme Verdurin guarantees, in effect, that such authority can be created by anyone. The identity and continuity of the nobility made it the sole measure of reality against which all else had to be compared, for the aristocracy alone was demonstrably real and could not be created. By replacing genealogy with a fiction, Mme Verdurin overturns the entire possibility of assurance, opening up the possibility that the absolute can be created, and the power to authenticate earned. Her triumph describes, then, not only the historical ascendance of the bourgeoisie but that of fiction over authenticity and the defeat of the principle of certainty. The flawless illusion, the disguise, is the axis on which this profanation turns and the means by which the counterfeit supplants the genuine without the chance of detection: Is judgement possible if fiction can forge even the grounds of authenticity?

Mme Verdurin camouflages the emptiness of her origins so artfully that she becomes indistinguishable from the "genuine" Princesse that Marcel knew. Discovery of her fraud will be virtually impossible, since the tradition of orderly succession has itself been marshalled to support her claim. Of course, such potential lay already in the aristocratic principle of repetition through change: "La succession au nom est triste comme toutes les successions, comme toutes les usurpations de propriété" (III, 955-56). She subverts the principle because "station" is no longer stationary, property is no longer one's own, but is handed over to another. That unique figure of the Princesse in whom Marcel had invested his grand vision of the nobility has lost her "proper meaning." In this countercurrent to the movement toward plenitude and meaning, all successions become usurpations for Marcel, and the uniqueness of the nobility disintegrates into a series of repetitions—at the very moment that the constant change in appearance that we have seen throughout the novel seems to climax in the "completed portraits" of the novel's characters. All along, Marcel has felt himself progressing toward a clearer sense of who each of these characters really is, but suddenly this movement explodes into an endless masquerade. In fact, this turns out to be no masquerade at all, but the parody of one, with people disguised as themselves. The final vision of the characters in the novel is of everyone in disguise. And if succession is indistinguishable from usurpation, the nobility has perhaps merely institutionalized the profanation of identity. Its history is the story of that fundamental discontinuity, but elevated into a principle of succession which can claim to preserve continuity. As Mme Verdurin's tactics have shown once again, the institutionalization of loss can become the denial of that loss; she is perhaps finally not essentially different from the "true aristocrats."

Yet Marcel's position here is paradoxical, for in isolating a moment of true value, he is committing the error of which he accuses the others at the final party. They see the present constellation of values as constant, but the narrator's own sense of devaluation and loss is founded on an identical nearsightedness: on the conviction that the aristocracy of his youth is the true source of *valeur*. It is a vision protected by memory, immune to his subsequent revelations. Any notion of real decline depends on a real *point de départ* from which the decline began. The devaluation is real only because Marcel takes his own past seriously. But it is real essentially *for him*, and it would be inadequate to see the decline of the nobility as merely an historical event or, as Bersani does, to view Marcel's reaction as simply "natural":

> [Marcel] naturally compares with sadness the beauty of the former princess with the vulgarity and ugliness of the ex-Mme Verdurin.... It is, of course, by no means the narrator's own snobbery that explains his regret for the closed aristocratic world of the past.6

This scene is not an expression of Marcel's snobbery, it is true, but neither is it an "objective" picture. It expresses, rather, Marcel's existential situation here, the loss of the authenticity for which he has been searching and of the possibility of certainty. Like Charlus confronted with Léa's letter to Morel, Marcel finds his entire frame of reference made suddenly precarious by a sense of sheer relativism. Paradoxically, even while he is stunned by the degradation of the nobility, he can see how perspective is a function of one's moment of entry:

> De changements produits dans la société je pouvais d'autant plus extraire des vérités importantes et dignes de cimenter une partie de mon œuvre qu'ils n'étaient nullement, comme j'aurais pu être au premier moment tenté de le croire, particuliers à notre époque. Au temps où, moi-même à peine parvenu . . . dans le milieu des Guermantes, j'avais dû y contempler, comme faisant partie intégrante de ce milieu, des éléments absolument différents, agrégés depuis peu et qui paraissaient étrangement nouveaux à de plus anciens dont je ne les différenciais pas . . . (III, 967)

Marcel, standing within the paradox of viewing change absolutely *and* relatively at the same time, gains an insight into the necessary structure of a work of fiction. He expresses once again the preservation of opposite alternatives within the story of change. Seeing himself in error, however, does not lead Marcel to avoid it, rather this culminates it, renewing the circle of error by completing it. Only in the totality of the work does the essential supplementarity become clear between the purity of the nobility and its corruption. The movements are interdependent, for the story of decline preserves the original illusion. Every loss of aura takes itself seriously, but recreates in the story of loss both the desired illusion and its demystification. Through the reader of the *Recherche*, it will be possible for Proust to attempt a strategy of recuperation which tries to use the story of Marcel's "undeceiving" to recreate the untenable illusion.

The efficacy of Marcel's error is confirmed by its repetition. In the process itself of transcending one illusion, he is arriving at another point of departure. Indeed, this loss of aura which he discovers at the Princesse's has occurred repeatedly in the novel. Through his readings, for one, Marcel knows this loss from Balzac, for whom the new nobility of the Empire was only a pale imitation of the true qualities of the *ancienne noblesse*. And already at the time of Louis XIV, Saint-Simon was complaining of the push of the *parvenus* and the generally growing ignorance of genealogy. Marcel acknowledges the age-old perpetuation of the loss of aura—a process surely as old as the nobility itself— when he points out that the legitimatization of social advancement was well demonstrated by the seventeenth-century practices whereby "le nom bourgeois d'un Colbert [est] devenu noble."[7] This *déception* has itself been experienced by Marcel much earlier. In his childhood, the drama of disappointment has already begun in the church of Combray.

Even before he sees her, the Duchesse de Guermantes fills Marcel's imagination as the magical link to the world of the stained-glass windows, bearer of the name which coincides with its object. When he sees her in church, his image is shattered: this figure which incarnates the authentic should above all make its presence immediately apparent. But the opposite occurs, and only by carefully piecing together all the bits of information and indications can Marcel *deduce* that the woman in the Guermantes pew, resembling what he knows of the Duchesse, is most likely Mme de Guermantes:

> [I]l ne pouvait vraisemblablement y avoir qu'une seule femme ressemblant au portrait de Mme de Guermantes, qui fût ce jour-là où elle devait justement venir, dans cette chapelle. (I, 174)

Instead of a flash of unmediated apprehension, there is only a slow and painfully subjective assemblage of evidence: the stuttering interposition of an unavoidable judgement. Having expected a figure "avec les couleurs d'une tapisserie ou d'un vitrail" with no similarity to the rest of humanity, Marcel is crushed:

> "C'est cela, ce n'est que cela, Mme de Guermantes!" . . . cette image qui naturellement n'avait aucun rapport avec celles qui, sous le même nom de Mme de Guermantes, étaient apparues tant de fois dans mes songes . . . [mais elle] était si réelle que tout, jusqu'à ce petit bouton qui s'enflammait au coin du nez, certifiait son assujetissement aux lois de la vie, comme dans une apothéose de théâtre un plissement de la robe de la fée, un tremblement de son petit doigt, dénoncent la présence matérielle d'une actrice vivante . . . (I, 175)

As in the experience of Mme Verdurin, the breakdown here is seen as a loss of continuity, no "connection" being found between the Duchesse and her image.

By not corresponding to it, she seems to make his image superfluous, a dislocation expressed as "overconcretization." The ethereal Duchesse is subjugated by her inescapable corporeality and made subject ("assujetir") to ordinary physical laws, her image betrayed ("dénoncer") by the material woman "inside." In this one moment of disappointment, the nobility becomes a role whose aura cannot fail to be destroyed by its particular manifestations, but the work of Marcel's imagination is only beginning at this point.

In the confrontation between his perception and his image, Marcel tries desperately to conceive a new ontological separation which will save the illusion. His image has foundered, however, not simply because the Duchesse has a ruddy face, but because she has *any* feature which can be described in terms applicable to other mere mortals or could belong to a certain "type féminin qui comprenait aussi des femmes de médecins et de commerçants" (I, 175).[8] Marcel tries first to shift the corruption of the image onto the "ignorance" of her body, but such a separation would turn the image into a "simple luminous projection," cut off from her essential reality. The image requires an operation of integration which reapplies the *idea* (of which his perception is now only a material manifestation) back upon the figure before him. His move precipitates a radical change in perspective, performing a leap. Rather than proceeding from the presumed authenticity of his image, Marcel now posits the integrity of the Duchesse *as he perceives her* as his point of departure:

> [M]ais cette Mme de Guermantes à laquelle j'avais si souvent rêvé, maintenant que je voyais qu'elle existait effectivement en dehors de moi, en prit plus de puissance encore sur mon imagination qui, un moment paralysée au contact d'une réalité si différente de ce qu'elle attendait, se mit à réagir et à me dire: "Glorieux dès avant Charlemagne . . . ." (I, 175-76)

In one move, Marcel has turned the initial defeat of his image into proof of the authenticity of the woman: the corporeality which first threatened the plausibility of the image has been transformed into its authentification. The structure of the experience recalls the "Confession d'une jeune fille"; the image of the girl's mother, created by anticipation and memory, cannot disappoint her, because the confrontation with the real person is structured to allow only the verification of the image's perfection in the form of discovery. Perception alone is never permitted to determine the character of reality. In Marcel's autonomous act of imagination here, the Duchesse is *perceived* as an expression of his idea and a confirmation of it. If his first reaction is disappointment and demystification, this imaginative perception enacts a "remystification." The *rapport* found lacking between the image and the perceived figure is retroactively restored, so that the original vision—and Marcel's expectations—may be verified:

> [J'essayais de garder le souvenir] de toutes ces particularités qui me semblaient autant de renseignements précieux, authentiques et singuliers sur son visage. Maintenant que me le faisait trouver beau toutes les pensées que j'y rapportais . . . la replaçant (puisque c'était une seule personne qu'elle et cette duchesse de Guermantes que j'avais évoquée jusque-là) hors du reste de l'humanité. . . . (I, 176)

Marcel's imagination has restored the wholeness and integrity of the world it encounters, finding the Duchesse immortal after all. Reinvested with her magic by his imagination, she once again evokes the image of the stained-glass window:

> Alors me rappelant ce regard qu'elle avait laissé s'arrêter sur moi, pendant la messe, bleu comme un rayon de soleil qui aurait traversé le vitrail de Gilbert le Mauvais. (I, 177)

Typically, however, his imagination conceals this operation as a *discovery* of unity: the Duchesse is found to be identical to his expectations. It is finally his imagination here which, like the ray of sunlight, shines through the figure of the Duchesse to reproduce the vision of the stained-glass window. In his retelling, Marcel perceives his initial disappointment as a mere mistake, a moment of confusion, so that like the aristocracy's assimilation of succession, the story of his loss becomes a refutation of that loss. The repetition of this drama suggests that perhaps the entire narrative of the *Recherche*, in one of its movements, is organized by such a structure of recuperation as we found in Proust's Ruskin essay. The loss of a mystified moment is recouped through an imaginative act of reinvestment and the retelling of the loss. As early as Proust's "Confession d'une jeune fille," we saw a story built around a repeated movement of loss and recovery, endlessly postponing the discovery of the imagination's role. The imaginative act saves Marcel's vision of the Duchesse, but part of its success is that in so doing, it hides from him the nature of the restitution. All trace of the "correction" of his original disappointment has disappeared, revealing Marcel in the position of the social novices meeting Mme Verdurin. The thrust of the text toward a moment of clarity, in a movement of progress toward self-knowledge, can be seen to be undermined, unwoven, Penelope-like, in the parallel drama of deception reenacted innumerable times.

We can now begin to see how a concert of such movements allows the work to extend itself and how this kind of experience serves as a paradigmatic structure for the novel as a whole. The narrative is constantly involved in concurrent projects of loss, recovery, concealment, and narration, reflecting the multi-directionality of all fiction. And the characters who themselves express and enact the workings of fiction, those, that is, who are metaphors for the textuality of the *Recherche* (Albertine, Mme Verdurin, Odette), are engaged in the same simultaneous movement of deception, loss, and illusory plenitude. The Duchesse in the church at Combray is likened to an actress, a metaphor suggesting the simultaneous "levels" of language, no one of which can alone describe the nature of the text. Albertine, too, will first be seen as "a great actress," and one whose beauty must similarly be restored by an act of Marcel's imagination:

> C'est parce que je l'avais vue comme un oiseau mystérieux, puis comme une grande actrice de la plage, désirée, obtenue peut-être, que je l'avais trouvée merveilleuse. Une fois captif chez moi l'oiseau . . . avait perdu toutes ses couleurs. . . . Elle avait peu à peu perdu sa beauté. (III, 173)

Only jealousy will inspire Marcel later to reinscribe in his image of Albertine the colors that first attracted him in order that he may rediscover in her that "iridescent actress of the beach":

> Il fallait des promenades comme celles-là, où je l'imaginais, sans moi, accostée par telle femme ou tel jeune homme, pour que je la revisse . . . [comme dans une première période] où elle était encore, quoique moins chaque jour, la chatoyante actrice de la plage. . . . (III, 173)

As it did in the church at Combray and with Albertine, Marcel's imagination must reestablish the connection ("rapport") which he finds missing between the world of his youth and the "coup de théâtre" of the final masquerade. Similarity of language reveals the parallel efforts being made; it is once again a question of "rediscovering" a continuity that Marcel is sure exists. When Marcel barely recognizes his host, the Prince de Guermantes, an intense intellectual effort is needed to ascertain his identity:

> A vrai dire je ne le reconnus qu'à l'aide d'un raisonnement et en concluant de la simple ressemblance de certains traits à une identité de la personne. (III, 921)

Since the entire notion of "identity" is in question here, it is even difficult to talk of recognition. Although Marcel eventually succeeds in relocating these figures in their history, they are repeatedly seen as so "different from themselves" that there is scant triumph for the principle of identification:

> En effet, "reconnaître" quelqu'un, et plus encore, après n'avoir pas pu le reconnaître, l'identifier, c'est penser sous une seule dénomination deux choses contradictoires . . . (III, 939)

They can be "identified" only by seeing them as they no longer are, "car on était obligé de les regarder, en même temps qu'avec les yeux, avec la mémoire" (III, 924). Only an elaborate and creative work of the imagination can abstract the essential "selves" of these people from their disguises.

This really represents a new dilemma for Marcel, for the principle of identity is being overthrown, it seems, just as Marcel is discovering himself as the only possible continuity between past and present. Only through memory can he establish what he perceives to be the essence of each character. It is no longer a question of investing Mme Verdurin with the aura of the Princesse: placing her among the nobility of the *vitrail* would only certify the destruction of his image of the old Princesse. It would turn her image into a figment of his imagination like his first anticipation of the Duchesse, an image "arbitrarily formed by me." He must try, rather, to *redefine* change as continuity, and succession as preservation. Marcel would restore the integrity of the nobility by redefining it as a role played by different actors at different times, but maintaining its own inherent character. His original point of contact, once seen as the only true image of the nobility stretching unbroken back to Charlemagne and Louis XIV, is now perhaps to be seen as only one among several possible vantage points. In this "garden" which the Guermantes line has become, individual flowers come and go, but the name remains intact.

> Ainsi, à tous les moments de sa durée, le nom de Guermantes . . . subissait des déperditions, recrutait des éléments nouveaux, comme ces jardins où à tout moment des fleurs à peine en bouton, et se préparant à remplacer celles qui se flétrissent déjà, se confondent dans une masse qui semble pareille, sauf à ceux qui . . . gardent dans leur souvenir l'image précise de celle qui ne sont plus. (III, 970)

Marcel seems to have saved the integrity of the nobility as a principle of constancy within change. The aristocracy has become a process of social evolution within which Mme Verdurin's rise is essentially no different from the rise, for example, of a Colbert:

> [Les changements produits dans la société] n'étaient nullement, comme j'aurais pu être au premier moment tenté de le croire, particuliers à notre époque. . . . Même dans le passé où je reculais le nom de Guermantes pour lui donner toute sa grandeur, et avec raison du reste, car sous Louis XIV les Guermantes, quasi royaux, faisaient plus grande figure qu'aujourd'hui, le phénomène que je remarquais en ce moment se produisait de même. Ne les avait-on pas vus alors s'allier à la famille Colbert par exemple, laquelle aujourd'hui, il est vrai, nous paraît très noble puisque épouser une Colbert semble un grand parti pour un La Rochefoucauld? Mais ce n'est pas parce que les Colbert, simples bourgeois alors, étaient nobles, que les Guermantes s'allièrent avec eux, c'est parce que les Guermantes s'allièrent avec eux qu'ils devinrent nobles. (III, 967)

Nevertheless, there remains something fundamentally inadequate, even contradictory, about Marcel's "solution," for it fails to admit the seriousness of the problem. It is not by turning the Guermantes into interchangeable figures that Marcel will preserve his vision of the nobility. Both these passages betray a regret felt through much of *Le Temps retrouvé*, a regret for that lost

Marcel's Fictional Project 95

vision. Rather than surrender it entirely, Marcel places the reality of that vision back in the irretrievable past. The flowers in his comparison only *seem* an undifferentiated mass—and only to those without a sense of history. They perpetuate themselves, maintaining an orderly succession, but a figure such as Mme Verdurin transgresses this order from the outside. Marcel's image finally offers him the nobility as a figure of no meaning or use to him and sacrifices both its grandeur and its purpose as a principle of authenticity. The Guermantes are never meant to be idle participants in the anonymous flow of the nobility; they are the yardstick by which that flow must be measured. The preservation of Marcel's vision will depend, as his regret itself implies, on memory and on the strategy of fiction, a strategy involved with both movements of deception and reinvestment, loss and recovery. The directions of ascent and decline will show themselves to be both necessary and even complementary. And a reading of Proust's novel will have to recognize that the numerous bourgeois intruders do not simply destroy Marcel's vision of the nobility; they are essential also in preserving that vision.

The process of desecration noticed at the final party insists on values which depend on a sense of *real* nobility. In order to perceive the travesty of Mme Verdurin as the Princesse de Guermantes, the reader is forced to admit the privileged nature of Marcel's first view of the aristocracy. Many of the characters of the novel are able to authenticate their status by creating a fictional history. Social climbing requires not only the ability to forge ahead but also the ability to forge a past. Mme Verdurin and Odette de Crécy are only the more adept practitioners of this art: Gilberte manages to cloud her past just as effectively as her mother did, while Jupien's niece finds the task performed for her by the society gossips after her marriage to "le petit Cambremer," and Bloch, in his old age, is able to give his present prestige "une sorte de recul indéfini." The retelling of the *Recherche* reverses this process, portraying the decline of the nobility in order to frame thereby the grandeur of the nobility that once existed. In detailing the bankruptcy of the present, Marcel's story describes a history of devaluation which affirms and preserves the glorious vision of the past. Balzac may have helped give Proust the means for articulating this transformation in his portrayal of Restoration high society. Suddenly the upper bourgeoisie were clothed in the rank and esteem that traditionally were the privilege of the feudal nobility. Roland Barthes has noted Balzac's agitation over this usurpation; the narrator of *Sarrazine* was appalled to discover that if you merely have enough money, no one will trouble himself about your origins.[9] The rights of the gentry, founded on tradition and verifiable lineage, have been taken over by the mercantilist class; the principle of the *entrepreneur*, the initiator *par excellence*, has replaced land and historical right as the source of social ordering. In terms Barthes borrowed from Peirce, money, which was only an *index* of distinction for the nobility, a mere attribute of power and station, is elevated by the bourgeoisie to the status of a *sign*. In these same terms, then, Marcel's act of narration can be seen as an attempt to reinvest the sign of the nobility with the force of an index, to restore the traces of origin to the image of the nobility. The decline Marcel witnesses is potentially more profound than Balzac's, for once his nobility has lost its privileged place as a source of authenticity, it has always been an empty sign. Reading through the masks at the Princesse's party, Marcel sees only the marks of the degeneration that has occurred since his youth, and he is seized with longing for the *valeur perdue* he once knew. It remains for him to discover the link between that vision of past fullness and his desire to appropriate that plenitude in the "sacred."

Everywhere in the novel, Marcel is committing the "error of literality," yielding to the temptation to seize his illusion, yet he is everywhere discovering his error and "correcting" himself. Each revelation seems only to justify another attempt, leading him into the recommission of his error, in another form perhaps. By the end of the novel, Marcel realizes this strategy is bringing him no closer either to his illusion of "pure essence" or to his vocation. After the party, it becomes clear that like Gérard in *Sylvie*, he cannot "return" to capture the lost vision of his youth, for it is inseparable from his memory of it. The image of pastness essential to his vision will only be rescued from its particular manifestation (what it has become) by a strategem which inscribes that vision ("what the nobility once was") in the story of its own demise. Proust's text forms the kind of "allegory" of experience, recapturing or resuscitating a past moment by describing its loss, that we found in his essays on Ruskin. The bourgeoisie will be revealed as the corrupters of true value and the usurpers of the mythical landed aristocracy in order to assure through Marcel's memory the authenticity of his original vision. This movement must remain implicit, for it constitutes a contingent authenticity dependent on the act of memory and narration. Marcel's key insight is structural: the grandeur of the nobility has always depended on its decline, and the sacred has always been "mixed" in its very nature. From the start, Marcel's image of the nobility arose through the social and spatial distance separating him from the Guermantes; to reestablish the vision, that distance must be reinscribed in the image through the distance of memory. Marcel takes sad notice of the vast *difference* between the pathetic figures he meets at the party and the grand ones he remembers:

> Rien n'est plus douloureux que cette opposition entre l'altération des êtres et la fixité du souvenir, quand nous comprenons que ce qui a gardé tant de fraîcheur dans notre mémoire n'en peut plus avoir dans la vie. (III, 987)

But it is precisely this play of difference which creates the "fraîcheur" of past images. It arises only through Marcel's memory, where the difference is established between the images of past and present. The failure of "la vie" will be turned into the triumph of "mémoire." The notion of simple pleasure has always been an illusion, discovered only in the troubled moment of loss. Like the "delicious trouble" of reading *Sylvie* or the impure pleasure of reading Ruskin in St. Mark's, Marcel's vision exists only in fiction and can only be maintained by the complex movements of a text. Such a text will trace the entire path he has followed so that the *fraîcheur* emerges through the recollection of a lost moment, in the indulgence of an idolatrous temptation, or through the juxtaposition of the real and the ideal, like the most vivid impression of involuntary memory:

> [J]e les éprouvais [ces diverses impressions] à la fois dans le moment actuel et dans un moment éloigné, jusqu'à faire empiéter le passé sur le présent, à me faire hésiter à savoir dans lequel des deux je me trouvais.... (III, 871)

Nerval showed Proust the need to commit the error of seizing an illusion, of attempting to return to a lost place; and the movement of the *Recherche* affirms that the path through error restores the lost vision which then appears to be the source of the text, like the woman Marcel conceives who is formed by his own appetite, but whom he imagines is actually the source of that temptation. Through memory, Marcel's narrative will re-create the nobility of his youth, seen in all its grandeur through aging eyes, and thus preserve an image which he no longer possesses—much as the essays on Ruskin were arranged to resurrect the lost image of Proust's infallible teacher and master. Marcel's quest is therefore a kind of repeated ritual invocation whose model was perhaps suggested by the "ritual profanations" of Mlle Vinteuil. In trying to create an image of evil, she succeeded in producing the opposite, for her act of profanation reveals for the narrator, perhaps more clearly than a conventional act of devotion, the "filial tenderness" which inspired it. The narration of the scene subordinates her intention to a narrative one and offers a striking example of how an image can be invoked by the spectacle of its desecration.

6

Conclusion: The Narrative Implications

The "sacred" quality Marcel recognized in the figure of Geneviève de Brabant and extended to the Guermantes is the irreplaceable contact with origin which demonstrates the clear and immediate being-there of the genuine, the area where name, place, and history coincide. If this essence which is its own authentification resists capture and refuses to be known directly, it can nevertheless invest the objects and persons with which it comes in contact with a mark of consecration. Marcel's constant quest for the authentic is closely linked to the search for his vocation, for somehow the genuine will guarantee the path to art, like the Duchesse de Guermantes, who Marcel imagines early on will offer him a special access to the secret of writing:

> Je rêvais que Mme de Guermantes m'y faisait venir, éprise pour moi d'un soudain caprice; tout le jour elle y pêchait la truite avec moi. Et le soir . . . elle me montrait le long des murs bas, les fleurs . . . et m'apprenait leurs noms. Elle me faisait lui dire le sujet des poèmes que j'avais l'intention de composer. (I, 172)

In telling him *how* to write, she will also put him in contact with the mythic dimension of the genuine and allow him to realize in language all the magic he found in the stained-glass windows. In terms of becoming a poet, he is reaching through her for a language which is full with the poetic intention, purely figurative, and liberated from materiality and accident.

The only access to this "wholeness" appears to be through a particularized form of the genuine, yet it seems always to become fragmented by detail. Marcel invariably finds the sacred only in a corrupted version, in the present moment, so he characteristically relocates the moment of purity and full potential back in the lost past. Just as he imagines a time—now forever lost to him—when he could have known the truth about Albertine, so his first encounter with the Duchesse reinserts the wholeness and sanctity of the nobility back in the mythic past. The urge to seize in the Duchesse the mythic quality that he saw in Geneviève de Brabant is analogous to the desire to possess in Albertine the vision inspired by the first glimpse of the *jeunes filles en fleurs*, the frieze by the sea. It might be said of Marcel what Gérard admitted in *Sylvie*, "C'est

Conclusion 99

une *image* qu'il poursuit." He would have the impossible chimera of an image, a name, a rhetorical figure, take on a form which would enable him to appropriate it. He imagines that a return to origins will yield the essence of the genuine, for the place of inception is privileged by an unobscured plenitude. In chasing Albertine or the Duchesse, Marcel is seeking a moment of original wholeness, perhaps the mythic goodnight kiss of his mother. In his attempt to seize the image "before" it was profaned, Marcel is led, not surprisingly, to pilgrimages to the site of the lost genuine. Hans-Robert Jauss has indicated that the novel can only relate *critically* to the mythic vision,[1] but Marcel's narrative efforts seem turned in the other direction as well, recalling a time when this was not yet the case. If this novel "began" with a journey to Ruskin's Amiens, it seems to complete itself in a pilgrimage of memory back into a fictional past, in a complex strategy aimed at recreating a lost vision—and thereby making it apparently once again viable.

The poetic project of freeing language from the constraints of its materiality and the accidents of everyday usage is, of course, hardly peculiar to Proust. Nerval showed, in his hermetic and elusive *Chimères*, a concerted effort to seize pure metaphoricity, and he even thematized this desire in the "pre-Adamites" of his fantastic prose. Mallarmé, similarly, saw poetry as an attempt to create a language exclusively to itself, while for Blake, sin seems to come into the world with the Creation, when the holy primordial essence is violated by a limiting incarnation into matter. Interestingly, in their studies of Proust, both Curtius and Jauss turn to the same quote from Flaubert which insists on the writer's need to emancipate his language from materiality:

> Je crois qu l'avenir de l'art est dans ces voies: . . . la forme en devenant habile s'atténue; elle quitte toute liturgie, toute règle, toute mesure . . . et est libre comme chaque volonté qui la produit. Cet affranchissement de la matérialité se retrouve en tout. . . . C'est pour cela qu'il n'y a ni beaux ni villains sujets, . . . le style étant à lui tout seul une manière absolue de voir les choses.[2]

One critic even found Proust's penchant for "glass" imagery an expression of the "ideal matter" of transparent language:

> C'est sans doute à eux [les maîtres-verriers] que [Proust] pense lorsqu'il affirme par exemple: "la matière de nos livres, la substance de nos phrases doit être immatérielle. . . .[3]

The means of expression would seem to become invisible, disappearing at the crucial moment—just as certain readers would have the bulk of the narrative evaporate into transparency once the final vision is achieved. Time and again, however, the project of transparency is frustrated or revealed to be essentially an illusion of language, a fiction. Like the image approached too closely, the key attempts at immediacy and appropriation are invalidated, for him, by a preoccupation with the particular. Marcel finally becomes convinced that the path of observation is futile, noting with disappointment that "Certes ce n'était pas des impressions de ce genre qui pouvaient me rendre l'espérance que j'avais perdue de pouvoir être un jour écrivain et poète, car elles étaient toujours liées à un objet particulier dépourvu de valeur intellectuelle et ne se rapportant à aucune vérité abstraite" (I, 179). Writing, the act of formulation itself, will come to seem a violation of "truth" or "essence," for once it is forced to take form, it is already profaned.

His first view of the Duchesse, then, cannot help but show Marcel the inevitable materiality beneath the veil of nobility. As Proust learned and as his novel shows, the attempt to use language—an attempt inseparable from the search for a pure language—is condemned continually to discover language's mixed nature. The project of finding a transparent language is not Proust's own, as Mendelson believes, but Marcel's.[4] When he encounters the mere person of the Duchesse in the church, his immediate attempt is to salvage his image of the nobility by purifying it of material contamination. As the text finds itself always "mixed" (an impure blend of literal and figural strands, accidental detail interwoven with metaphoric microcosm, realism and rhetoric), Marcel's subsequent—and successful—response is to assimilate the contradictions in the figure of the Duchesse. Marcel manages to integrate the difference between what he imagined and what he finds into an affirmation of his vision, making (or discovering) the profane to be part of the sacred. To illustrate art's "mixed essence," Geoffrey Hartman has cited a Kafka parable that is relevant here:

> Leopards break into the temple and drink the sacrificial chalices dry; this occurs repeatedly, again and again, finally it can be reckoned on beforehand and becomes part of the ceremony.[5]

"Profanation enters the inner sanctum and becomes part of the holy," Hartman explains, but the parable, like Proust's text, goes even further, demonstrating that fiction entails the institutionalization of the profane into the sacred. The language revealed by the text of the *Recherche* is not clear and transparent, but a medium on the verge of transparency, a kind of translucent substance whose opacity is necessary to maintain the essential difference that makes possible the interplay of its elements. The failure to find a transparent language is rather part of the plan of the novel, recalling the image produced at Marcel's early trip to the Vivonne. The unique *fraîcheur* of the image there, the exchange of predicates, is expressed by the bottles in the stream which create the exciting interplay between their apparent transparency and their evident presence.

The reader is surely meant to discover the play of oppositions which build the text of the *Recherche*. This is reflected in the compound vocabulary

Conclusion

which numerous critics feel compelled to use to describe the work. For Blanchot, we recall, this is "une œuvre achevée-inachevée," and for Benjamin, a "Penelope-work" both of recollection and forgetting; Barthes found the text arising from two discourses juxtaposed—the "encoder" and the "décoder," while for Genette, the most troubling aspect of the *Recherche* is that "elle se présente à la fois comme œuvre et comme approche de l'œuvre."[6] All share the sense of a disturbing *simultaneity* of directions in the novel. By "Marcel" we designate the project which aims to know the sacred directly, hoping to seize a clear vision of the world by possessing in the particular woman—or city, or work of art—the figure he imagined there. If the narrative only *seems* to "come out" somewhere and arrive at Marcel's success, it is because this view reflects only one perspective on the narrator's experience. His project, however, must be seen in the context of the narrative whole which seems to acknowledge the impossibility of these projects. In this sense, the attempt we noted earlier to structure the beginning and the end of the novel so that the whole can be "contained" is really a "Marcellian" project, a vestige of the irresistible urge to control the entire movement of the text. It is not in the nature of the *Recherche*, seen as a whole made up of opposing directions interacting, to resolve, finally, the disorientation and discomfort of the reader. On the contrary, the novel's manner of composition shows the body of the work, "tout 'l'entre-deux,' " constantly escaping the preconceived boundaries which its author had prepared. He was continually forced to elaborate Marcel's adventures, trying to follow all paths and encompass all the implications of the paths already followed.

Proust's narrative must continue to be read as a complex of simultaneous movements, and if we cannot fail to notice the tendency in the final pages of the *Recherche* for the narrator to "sum up" its achievement, that attempt must be placed back in the intentional context of the narrative. Just at the point where "Marcel" and "Proust" seem about to converge, the reader is struck by the increasing tension between their positions—between "Marcel's" urge to state clearly what the narrative has accomplished and "Proust's" accumulated indications through the narrative that such directness and clarity are unrealistic. "Marcel" appears tempted to formulate directly what the work has achieved and by so doing to "declare" its completion. At the same time, paradoxically, he seems to arrive at the understanding that the essence of a work of art is hidden and must be deciphered by each individual: "Ce qui était clair avant nous n'est pas à nous" (III, 880). His own interpretations of the narrative will not do; the reader must decipher their significance for himself. There are even declarations against direct statements and admissions of a certain failure: "Des impressions telles que celles que je cherchais à fixer ne pouvaient que s'évanouir au contact d'une jouissance directe" (III, 877). And although he concedes that "une œuvre où il y a des théories est comme un objet sur lequel on laisse la marque du prix" (III, 882), he cannot seem to resist offering the privileged "message" of his novel. If the presence of these theories which seek to short-circuit the circuitous path of the *Recherche*, like the price tag, confesses an inadequacy which must be supplemented, it is then possible—even necessary—to ask what strategy is revealed by the strange juxtapositions of this final volume.

An understanding of this strategy is facilitated considerably by recalling the project Proust discovered in his reading of *Sylvie*. Gérard, the main character, is engaged there in an attempt to recover from his insanity as well as to recover his childhood innocence. His solution is to return to the countryside of his memory, hoping to find there the simple, innocent life he remembers in the person of the girl Sylvie. But Gérard's disease, as Proust pointed out in his essay, is the radical disorientation which makes it impossible for him to distinguish clearly between the worlds of fiction and reality. Gérard's projects of recovery are thus working at cross-purposes, for the disorientation which seems to make possible the illusory recovery of his childhood innocence is itself the disease that prevents his return to sanity. Gérard can never actually reach the point of recovery, but this failure allows him to succeed in producing the most enchanting but dangerous image of recovery in his vision of the Valois. Like the narrator of "La Confession d'une jeune fille," the fiction he produces—the story of the loss he imagines—*replaces* the impossible recovery.[7] If "Marcel" is the aspect of the text which is striving for transparency, "Proust" is the voice which admits its impossibility. Instead of giving up the attempt, however, with this admission, he integrates both the project and its failure into his text. In involuntary memory, Proust has discovered the means of "recovering" his lost world, even while preserving the distance which is the source of its special value. The Combray of his childhood with his first vision of the Duchesse de Guermantes will be recaptured—but only for Marcel. As the attempt for transparency and presence must fail, which Proust well knows, he must create a surrogate voice, Marcel, who can pursue this objective in all "sincerity." Only by this means can Proust "recoup" his losses, developing Marcel's failure into a complex strategy to recapture, if not the sacred itself, then a *vision* of the sacred. Fiction alone offers the language through which this crucial distance can be maintained. In this case, nothing could demonstrate more convincingly the importance for Proust's text to preserve Marcel's errors. Like his introduction to Ruskin, Proust's *Recherche* is also the story of misreading and an allegory of error.

The image of a "nearly transparent" medium, like the image of the bottles lying in the Vivonne, embodies the history of the attempt to overcome the distance of imagination and desire, the failure of that attempt, and the act of synthesis which turns this history into the work of art. Marcel's first sight of the Duchesse similarly contains the diachronic history of the nobility[8] as well as the history of Marcel's relationship to that nobility; that first image comprehends his urge toward the visionary purity of Geneviève de Brabant and his subsequent discovery of the "présence matérielle" of the Duchesse. As in the Kafka parable, the profane reveals itself to be part of—and even the means to—the sacred: the time lost by Marcel in the salons of the Faubourg Saint-Germain is also the means of recovering that lost time by furnishing him the material of his novel. The work as a whole, in evoking the vision of an uncorrupted, "prehistoric" aristocracy, suggests even that it is the act of profanation which opens up the possibility of the sacred. The act of writing, which appeared to corrupt the authentic, reveals itself in addition as the transgression which guarantees the special nature of the object it appears to destroy. The movement into fiction becomes a kind of invocation which opens the middle ground where the vision has not yet been fragmented. It is still intact, like those mornings Proust found in Nerval which sustain within them the "delicious colors" of possibility:

> Telles sont ces matinées bénies, creusées (par une insomnie, l'ébranlement nerveux d'un voyage, une ivresse physique, une circonstance exceptionnelle) dans la dure pierre de nos journées, et gardant miraculeusement les couleurs délicieuses, exaltées, le charme de rêve qui les isole dans notre souvenir comme une grotte merveilleuse, magique et multicolore dans son atmosphère spéciale. (*CSB*, p. 239)

Mme Verdurin describes the corruption of the nobility, but the story of her sacrilege proves the integrity of the "real" Princesse de Guermantes.

Marcel's search is "motivated" by a repetition, ritual in character, that he witnesses in the window at Montjouvain, creating the image of purity through an act of desecration. In order to be efficacious, that which is to be consecrated must be *ritually* destroyed.[9] In this way, each disillusionment permits, even necessitates, the beginning again which its finality seems to deny, the sacrifice assuring the possibility of resurrecting the image of the "sacred." The attempt to achieve a mastery over the loss of the vision by repeating the story of that loss is also reminiscent of Proust's early narrative, "La Confession d'une jeune fille." Marcel has become a key part of a strategy for rekindling that vision— which is not to imply that Proust has escaped the seduction of the text. On the contrary, his use of a character suspiciously like himself, but one who can pursue the idolatrous project with apparent sincerity, implicates Proust in that project. Through this strategy, he reveals his involvement in the attempt to recover a lost plenitude—of language or experience—which the countercurrents of his novel, as we have seen, insist is not authentically possible. The attempt to be both reader and writer of the text involves Proust once again in the desire to "have it both ways." The strategic organization of the text suggests that Marcel's idolatry is Proust's response to his own sense of bad faith. Writing *means* becoming entangled in the idolatrous temptations of the text. His repeated attempts to seize Albertine remind us also of another ritual in the novel, the drama of going to bed which played itself out in the nights of

Marcel's Combray childhood. As in that ceremony, repetition of the thrust toward possession of his mistress is made possible only by the daily forgetting of the previous night's disillusionment, revealing this, as Walter Benjamin recognized, as much a novel of forgetting as of remembering. Marcel is a Scheherazade, finding in the morning following each unsuccessful attempt at transcendence the forgetfulness necessary to repeat his Sisyphean efforts. And like Scheherazade, it is the repetition which enables the narrative to continue. Marcel's days are like those of his youth that began with sheer joy because they were cut off from the memory of the anguish experienced the night before and thus were free of trepidation of the night to come:

> Et cet état [d'angoisse] durerait jusqu'au lendemain, quand . . . je sauterais à bas du lit pour descendre vite au jardin, sans plus me rappeler que le soir ramènerait jamais l'heure de quitter ma mère. (I, 183)

For Marcel, forgetfulness and repetition create, again and again, the possibility of possession. By eradicating the experience of disillusion and wiping out the traces of profanation, the ritual is continually postulating a time "before" the Fall, "before" the corruption of language, and thereby forever recreating the possibility of wholeness. In the story of its loss, the vision becomes real once more, because it is imaginable. Although the attempt at appropriation fails time and again, recounting the story of that discovery replaces the lost aura in the image of the past. The strategy of the novel reveals Marcel as an instrument in Proust's urge to master the complex movements of the text in order to restore the "vision claire" and the possibility of sure judgement, both of which are denied by the narrator's experience in the novel. The tone of *Le Temps retrouvé* betrays a desire to privilege one aspect of that experience and give it an authoritative interpretation of the whole. In light of the irreducible complexity of the text, it is necessary to place its final pages in perspective.

There is an essential difference to be noted between the vision Marcel has sought and that which is redeemed. The image of the Duchesse after Marcel has seen her in church is not the same as before that experience, and Mme Verdurin is surely not the Princesse de Guermantes. The image reborn through the imaginative act in the narrative is never identical to that which precedes it— and this difference is precisely what is accomplished by the narration. The reader is never permitted to arrive at a single, final meaning. The "story" is never "complete," since it is itself a story of differentiation. Nor is the *Recherche* the same novel as that toward which Marcel has directed his search— although his language would often have us believe this is the case. Even Proust found that kind of control escaping him. Toward the end of the novel the narrator explains, "[A]ujourd'hui tous ces fils différents s'étaient réunis pour faire la trame" (III, 972), as though he would tie up all the many threads of his

Conclusion

narrative into a single moment of ultimate coherence and purpose, into a single woven image:

> Une simple relation mondaine, même un objet matériel, si je le retrouvais au bout de quelques années dans mon souvenir, je voyais que la vie n'avait pas cessé de tisser autour de lui des fils différents qui finissaient par le feutrer de ce beau velours inimitable des années, pareil à celui qui dans les vieux parcs enveloppe une simple conduite d'eau d'un fourreau d'émeraude. (III, 973)

By stepping into the role of novelist, Marcel is trying to make claims for his experience beyond the perspective of a mere character. But the final impressions left by the novel must be reconsidered in the perspective drawn by the whole.

Portions of *Le Temps retrouvé*, like the passage just cited, find Marcel claiming to offer in one image an expression of the final sense of his journey, the meaning of all the paths he has taken. The many encounters throughout his life with the people he now sees in their old age, the many different aspects and appearances they presented on the way, now would all appear to be just so many accidental contours of the terrain he has covered:

> Plus d'une des personnes que cette matinée réunissait ou dont elle m'évoquait le souvenir, me donnait les aspects qu'elle avait tour à tour présentés pour moi . . . comme un accident de terrain . . . révèle ainsi au voyageur des changements d'orientation et des différences d'altitude dans la route qu'il suit. (III, 970)

Now that he feels he has reached his vocation, it seems to Marcel that he has gained a transcendent overview of his past and can look back and take in the entire path he has traveled. It is as though he has finally created the total context in which to place his experience, allowing him at last to lend it a final—and now definitive—interpretation:

> En remontant de plus en plus haut, je finissais par trouver des images d'une même personne séparées par un intervalle de temps si long, conservées par des moi si distincts . . . qu'il me fallait le hasard d'un éclair d'attention pour les rattacher. (III, 970-71)

We are seeing here the "reapplication" of the idea to Marcel's image, something we first saw in the church at Combray. But the novel, in its *process*, has always been insisting that its nature is revealed no less by its diachronic history than by its synchronic moments. The story, however, is more than its conclusion, nor is it to be completely determined by its outcome. Such privileging of the "result" of his search would totally rob of significance all the accidents and particulars of his path, in opposition to the sense the novel has created that the path is the outcome. Jauss has even characterized the originality of the *Recherche* by its refusal to clarify the action through a "Vogelperspektiv."[10] Roger Shattuck has also discussed this key image in order to refute Joseph Frank's apparent desire to privilege Proust's spatial metaphor (in *The Widening Gyre*).[11] Shattuck has perceived that the fundamental double movement of the text must be appreciated, but he nevertheless fails to grasp how essentially *textual* this complexity is. The panoramic view from above to which Marcel pretends is part of his general effort in the novel's closing pages to sum up the result of his journey. He would *define* its meaning and give the path he has been tracing a retroactive directionality. He would "take stock" of the work and "account for" the preceding complexity, dissipating that complexity in order to locate and master, finally, the direction in which all these experiences and transformations have been heading. The language of the last chapters aims at verifying the experience of the novel by giving it a definitive sense, suggesting that the experience of the search would be meaningless or incomprehensible without a clear explanation of the *point d'arrivée*. But in fact, it is the end of the *Recherche* which is incomprehensible without an understanding of the places Marcel has been in his development, both physically and spiritually. The refusal to take the bird's-eye view, which Jauss noticed, indicates the *text's* acknowledgment of the need to enact itself. As each redefinition is only part of the process, no single development—even in the novelist's voice at the end of the work—can hope to redefine the entire work. Nor can the final moments of Marcel's journey transcend its history. The reading of the *Recherche* has shown that to appreciate its complex nature, the work of fiction must be allowed to weave its own course. Without its history, the work becomes "anonymous," like the mass of indistinguishable flowers the Guermantes become. Without a sense of the constant interplay among its movements, the text appears to be a linear voyage, passing only negligible obstacles on the way to truth.

The contradictions of the final pages must be fitted back into the whole of the novel. Marcel, for instance, can hardly ever be accepted in the terms and perspective in which he sees or presents himself; indeed, self-deception is in character for him. As the novel has demonstrated, Marcel is often at quite a different point in his development and in a different situation than he believes or realizes. In his crucial experience with Albertine, we might observe that he is most fully in contact with her true nature at the moment when he seems least to appreciate her essence. In insisting that she *can* be circumscribed and controlled, that is, at the moment when he is most clearly evading the illimitable nature of her textuality, Marcel is in fact confronting her elusive textual nature most directly. For only in that earnest confrontation of deception does Albertine's real essence emerge: she reveals herself only when she is eluding Marcel, because her nature lies in her quintessential elusiveness. Marcel's unique role as narrator arises from his ability to reveal through his language and experiences what he has not yet discovered himself. Often this ignorance or blindness is precisely what enables the revelation to come forth and is essential to his function in the novel. The unity of Balzac's *Comédie humaine*, we recall, was verified for Proust by the fact that it was *discovered* by the author in his work, and only after much of the writing had been completed. The integrity and organic harmony of the whole is genuine because it grew out of the work itself instead of being imposed by the author upon the work in its plan. Balzac's novel shows "[une] unité qui s'ignorait, donc vitale et non logique" (III, 161), a unity, so to speak, unintentional, which assures the authenticity of the whole. In Proust's *plan*, however, as his correspondence clearly stated, he tried to build a structure which would assure this unity in advance. The only way remaining, then, for the novel to claim this authenticity is through Marcel, who is by definition ignorant of the structure of the enterprise in which he is engaged. The theoretical clarifications which abound in *Le Temps retrouvé* try to explain how Marcel reached his vocation, but they are also an attempt to circumscribe the significance of the narrator's experience, to appropriate the preceding text, and in this manner they betray the desire, implicit in the entire strategy of the novel, to control the whole of the work. This desire is, of course, part of the whole, only the reader must not forget that Marcel's urge to gain an overview of his experience discloses the desire to have these events "à la fois" and under control, *rather than* experienced "tour à tour." The "Vogelperspektiv" is analogous, on the level of the whole novel, to Marcel's attempt to surround and possess all of Albertine's secrets and hidden meanings.

 The text, however, resists the attempt to control it either through Marcel's overview or through the author's preexisting strategy. It overflows the strategy, rather, containing it instead of being contained in it. If Marcel would locate an image of his journey through the *Recherche*, he will find it by reconsidering the figure he has chosen. It does not lie in the "snapshot" he imagines of the carpet as a finished product, a ready vindication of his "climb"; it must be seen in another perspective. The carpet that is this novel is constantly being woven and rewoven, as though Scheherazade were fashioning an oriental carpet, and it is the endless process of interweaving that builds the fascinating complexity of the novel. Its contradictions are perhaps a necessary part of the whole, but the story must be read both "à la fois" and "tour à tour," in the weaving and unweaving of a contrapuntal structure of which the final pattern is only one aspect. The story is one of continual redefinition; events, impressions, and interpretations are forever being recapitulated and recast in new perspectives so that they comment on, redefine, and even parody the earlier appearance. As clarification is always an indication of a previous oversight or blindness, it is justifiable to ask whether the final interpretation offered escapes from this process.

 To this end, Marcel's final, great illumination of the novel must be reexamined in the context created by the party at the Princesse de Guermantes's. The "coup de théâtre" in the Guermantes salon, where the narrator sees his former acquaintances suddenly many years older, giving him a sense of time made concrete and "exteriorized," takes place in the afterglow of his instance of enlightenment in the courtyard. There, in his famous experience of standing on two unequal paving stones, Marcel finds himself back in a previous moment in time when he first stood before St. Mark's in Venice, and he feels a great ecstasy in the sudden juxtaposition of past and present, "à la fois dans le présent et dans le passé," where sights and smells are "reéls sans être actuels, idéaux sans être abstraits" (III, 872-73). Clearly, this is a moment of privileged existence, when Marcel seems to partake in reality of the impossible juxtaposition that belongs only to the world of imagery. It is the experience of pure existence, of impossible simultaneity of particular and general, distance and possession, that Marcel has fantasized throughout the novel. This epiphany is followed by the lengthy theoretical passages of *Le Temps retrouvé*, for this experience has lent Marcel the insight necessary for his task as a writer. He feels it has revealed to him the true nature of his past and clarified how he must proceed toward his novel. It seems to vindicate for him the time he has lost in the past by giving him the key to redeeming that past through art. In his greatest moment, Marcel finally comes upon the essence of time, "un peu de temps à l'état pur" (III, 872).

The traditional reading of this now classic experience of *mémoire involontaire* finds this the climax of Proust's novel: Marcel recovers the essence of the past and knows time in a "pure state" through the *déjà vu* evoked by the paving stones. Thrown between the poles of past and present, he transcends ordinary temporality, an experience which guarantees him his vocation. Such an interpretation forgets, however, that this is Marcel's *intentional* version of the event and that it bespeaks his desire to formulate the successful completion of his project. In actuality, Marcel is most mystified at this point which is generally considered the height of his enlightenment. The nature of this text will emerge only from an integration of that experience with the *déjà vu* that follows inside the salon and to which it is, in some sense, a prelude. For the novel is written in counterpoint, and the overture played in the Guermantes courtyard is recapitulated in a different mode at the party inside. The text does not end with Marcel's intention, but continues beyond it: in the scene following his illumination, the sight of friends in their old age is portrayed as a *travestissement* of his original perception of them. The guests are a grotesque disguise of their former selves, just as this party is a parody of the preceding transcendent experience of time. The discovery of the past in the present, which in the courtyard was the isolation of "un peu de temps à l'état pur," here finds itself, like the proud M. d'Argencourt, "peint en caricature" (III, 924). Time, the glorious medium of the first moment, is exteriorized here in d'Argencourt's horrible and disfiguring wrinkles; the clarity of that experience

Conclusion

is mirrored by the distortion time offers in the later version. Much as the homosexual "ending" of many of the novel's characters is more a continuation of their metamorphosis and a disappearance into a perennial mask than a clear and definitive identification of their true selves, so the novel ends not in a final clarity and identity, but in a proliferation of identities. In the terms of the mask image, each character becomes no more reduced to an identity than a succession of masks, characterized rather by their ability to defeat all expectation, and never quite surrendering their *imprévu* and their ability to act unforeseeably. Just as the narrator's certainty that he is about to seize the mystery of Albertine must be seen in light of the subsequent realization that he was closest to grasping her essence when she was slipping away from him, so must Marcel's achievement of his vocation be replaced in perspective. The text never gives up its context.

The only clear direction at the end seems to be toward Marcel's novel, but the clarity is itself misleading. The structure of the novel entails a fundamental *renversement*, which is to say that the "change in movement" that readers see in the final book is occurring throughout the narrative. Even while Marcel is struggling toward his work, the work within which he is contained is accomplishing itself. For Marcel to reach his vocation, instead of being a judge, a reader, a decoder trying to reach the intentional center of the evidence, he must become the weaver of a network, the postulator of the fictional center from which the particulars appear to emanate. The work acts as a kind of mirror, reflecting back through its own history to a "past" which it redefines and in which it is itself defined. But as the juxtaposition of the episodes here has shown, the narrative is not simply one side of the phenomenon of reflection, but *both sides*. To create such a work, Marcel must learn to don the mask of fiction, which means rejecting the simplistic notion of a single, true identity which the mask hides. He must prepare rather "cent masques qu'il convient d'attacher à un même visage" (III, 1045), of which he adds, "la nécessité, si on veut peindre le réel, a pu apparaître au cours de ce récit . . : . " The novel "succeeds" at the end—but in terms in which it has been succeeding *all through* the work, in terms, that is, of the mask. Unable to recover the mythic plenitude he imagines or to recapture a vision of it, Marcel will nevertheless resurrect—through the story of his search—the possibility that such recovery is feasible. Simultaneously, of course, it will be demystifying that possibility. By creating Marcel, the novel creates both "Proust" *and* "Marcel"; and as Marcel's itinerary is at every point both reflective and prefigurative, the text creates the simultaneity of starting out and arriving that Blanchot called the "finished-unfinished work." As Marcel's image along the Vivonne foresaw, the voices of the text's origin exchange places interminably, with Marcel the character becoming the apparent source of the text, yet remaining still caught in the contents of that text. It was this multipolarity of the text's fictional origin that juxtaposed the incompatible elements of Nerval's narrative and inspired in Proust the "delicious trouble" that charmed and excited him in *Sylvie*. For the reader, too, there is no completion, only the less blinded return to his earlier encounters with the text.

Notes

Introduction

1 J. M. Cocking, *Proust* (London: Bowes and Bowes, 1956), p. 118.

2 Whether or not Proust intended to keep "Marcel" as the narrator's name has by now become an important subject of discussion. Michihiko Suzuki—"Le 'je' proustien," *Bulletin de la Société des Amis de Marcel Proust*, 9 (1959), 69-82—and Harold Waters—"The Narrator, not Marcel," *French Review*, 33 (Feb. 1960), 389-92—have argued convincingly that Proust was in the process of effacing that name from the text when he died. If I persist in this now traditional use of "Marcel" interchangeably with "the narrator," it is because I believe the potential confusion of identities (author/character), which is based on the narrative "je" and exploited by the use of the name "Marcel," is part of Proust's deliberate effort to disorient the reader. In any event, one would always want to distinguish carefully between the narrator or character, Marcel, and the biographical author, Marcel Proust.

3 Paul de Man, "Proust et l'allégorie de la lecture," in *Mouvements premiers* (Paris: Corti, 1972), p. 232.

4 *A la recherche du temps perdu*, ed. Pierre Clarac and André Ferré (Paris: Gallimard, 1954), I, 166-67. All further references indicate the volume and page of this three-volume Pléiade edition. © Editions Gallimard. Used by permission.

5 Jean-Pierre Richard, in his *Proust et le monde sensible* (Paris: Seuil, 1974), examined the erotic components of its "fraîcheur" and its link to Mme de Guermantes, while Paul de Man (see note 3 above) and Gérard Genette—"Métonymie chez Proust," in *Figures III* (Paris: Seuil, 1972)—have explored the "rhetorical strategy" of the image of the carafes. Most recently, Philippe Lejeune has published a lengthy study of this passage, focusing especially on the way the image transcends the limits of the experience and achieves "une réalisation partielle d'un désir: celui de la métonymie généralisée"—"Les Carafes de la Vivonne," *Poétique*, No. 31 (Sept. 1977), p. 286.

6 Genette, p. 54.

7 Cf. Louis Hjelmslev, *Prolegomena to a Theory of Language*, trans. F. J. Whitfield, 2nd ed. (Madison: University of Wisconsin Press, 1963), esp. pp. 38-39.

8 Edward Said, *Beginnings* (New York: Basic Books, 1975), p. 163.

9 Said, p. 163.

10 De Man, p. 240.

11 De Man, p. 238.

12 From the essay "Notes sur la littérature et la critique," in *Contre Sainte-Beuve*, ed. Pierre Clarac and Yves Sandre, Bibliothèque de la Pléiade (Paris: Gallimard, 1971), p. 304n. All further references will be indicated by *CSB*. © Editions Gallimard. Used by permission.

13 Cf. Friedrich Schlegel's famous observation that Romantic poetry (by which he means poetic language) only seems to fulfill itself in its concrete manifestation, but actually always "floats" between its apparent intention (the "real") and its apparent source (the "ideal"), in Schlegel, *Kritische Schriften*, ed. W. Rasch (Munich: Hanser, 1956), p. 37.

14 From the essay "Gérard de Nerval," *CSB*, p. 234, and cited again by Proust in "La Méthode de Sainte-Beuve," *CSB*, p. 224.

15 Said, p. 244.

16 In this vein, one can talk also of Swann "reading his world," and John Lapp has worked out an interesting instance of Swann misreading Odette—"Proust's Windows to Reality," *Romanic Review*, 67 (Jan. 1976), 38-49—while Gilles Deleuze has presented the entire *Recherche* as a kind of semiotic *Bildungsroman—Marcel Proust et les signes* (Paris: P. U. F., 1970).

17 Yet, as Georges Poulet has noted in *L'Espace proustien* (Paris: Gallimard, 1963) and as the opening passages of *Combray* confirm, Marcel is quite uncomfortable without a firm orientation. The artist Elstir, on the other hand, thrives in this position, exploiting the lack of definition and finding in ambiguity the source of his art: "[Elstir] s'était au contraire attaché à ces traits d'ambiguité comme à un élément esthétique qui valait d'être mis en relief" (I, 849). Allan Pasco has also explored the double edge of Proust's ambiguity in his *Color-Keys to "A la recherche du temps perdu"* (Geneva: Droz, 1976), especially pp. 26-32.

18 Genette, "Proust palimpseste," in *Figures* (I) (Paris: Seuil, 1966), p. 67.

19 See Charles Peirce, "Logic as Semiotic: The Theory of Signs," in *The Philosophy of Peirce*, ed. Justus Buchler (London: K. Paul, Trench, Trubner, 1940), p. 100.

20 Gaëtan Picon, *Lecture de Proust* (Paris: Mercure de France, 1963), pp. 9-10.

21 Benjamin, "Zum Bilde Prousts," in *Illuminationen* (Frankfurt-am-Main: Suhrkamp, 1961), pp. 355-56; trans. Harry Zohn as *Illuminations* (New York: Schocken, 1969), p. 202.

22 Barthes, "Proust et les noms," in *To Honor Roman Jakobson* (The Hague: Mouton, 1967), p. 154.

23 De Man, " 'New criticism' et nouvelle critique," *Preuves*, No. 188 (Oct. 1966), p. 35.

24 Maurois, *A la recherche de Marcel Proust* (Paris: Hachette, 1949), p. 7.

25 Picon, p. 10.

26 Rousset, *Forme et signification* (Paris: Corti, 1962), p. 165.

27 Jauss, *Zeit und Erinnerung in Marcel Prousts "A la recherche du temps perdu"* (Heidelberg: Carl Winter, 1955), a work unfortunately not yet available in English or French.

28 An observation Proust made earlier in "Sainte-Beuve et Balzac," *CSB*, p. 274.

29 See Benjamin Crémieux, *Du côté de chez Marcel Proust* (Paris: Lemarget, 1929), Ch. 5, and cited in Jean-Yves Tadié, *Proust et le roman* (Paris: Gallimard, 1971), p. 245.

30 To Paul Souday, 17 Dec. 1919, cited in Tadié, p. 245.

31 *Les Plaisirs et les jours*, reprinted in the Pléiade edition of *Jean Santeuil*, ed. Pierre Clarac and Yves Sandre (Paris: Gallimard, 1971), p. 85. All further references will be indicated by *JS*. © Editions Gallimard. Used by permission.

32 Doubrovsky, *La Place de la madeleine* (Paris: Mercure de France, 1974), p. 96.

33 Doubrovsky, p. 98. This ostensible "identification" through the text of the reader with Proust's narrative "je" is the hypothesis that Suzuki has put forward to justify the complete elimination of the name "Marcel," cf. Suzuki, p. 81.

34 Cf. Picon, pp. 191 ff., Gide in his *Journal* (Paris: Gallimard, 1951), p. 1322, and especially Albert Feuillerat, *Comment Marcel Proust a composé son roman* (New Haven: Yale University Press, 1934), passim.

Chapter 1: The Pilgrimage: Proust Reads Ruskin

1 From the essay "Ruskin à Notre-Dame d'Amiens," published in April 1900 and reprinted in *Pastiches et mélanges* (Paris: Gallimard, 1919) as "Journées de pèlerinage." With another essay from 1900, it forms the body of the preface to Proust's translation of *La Bible d'Amiens*. As all Proust's articles on Ruskin now appear in the Pléiade *Contre Sainte-Beuve*, all references will be made to that edition.

2 Jean Autret, *L'Influence de Ruskin sur la vie, les idées et l'œuvre de Marcel Proust* (Geneva: Droz, 1955), p. 65.

3 General accounts of Proust's relationship to Ruskin can be found in George Painter, *Marcel Proust: A Biography*, 2 vols. (London: Chatto and Windus, 1959-65), René de Chantal, *Marcel Proust: Critique littéraire*, 2 vols. (Montreal: University of Montreal Press, 1967), and Walter Strauss, *Proust and Literature* (Cambridge: Harvard University

Press, 1957). In addition to *L'Influence de Ruskin*, Autret has coauthored, with William Buford, a translation of "Sur la lecture" with a long introductory essay, *On Reading* (New York: Macmillan, 1971). Other works devoted to Ruskin's influence on Proust include Sybil de Souza, *L'Influence de Ruskin sur Proust* (Montpellier: Manufacture de la charité, 1932), and Henri Lemaître, *Proust et Ruskin* (Toulouse: Privat-Didier, 1944). Barbara Harlow has recently published an interesting piece, "Sur la lecture," which is based on Proust's essay and examines reading as an act of translation, in *Modern Language Notes*, 90 (1975), 849-71.

[4] Strauss, p. 184. Proust's translation is dedicated to the memory of his father, yet it is possible that animosity he concealed toward his biological father was expressed in an explicit repudiation of his spiritual father, Ruskin. In addition, as Proust reminds us, Ruskin conceived *The Bible of Amiens* as part of a tetralogy, *Our Fathers Have Told Us*.

[5] Painter, II, 8-10.

[6] Proust continues, "Ainsi, j'ai essayé de pourvoir le lecteur comme d'une mémoire improvisée" (*CSB*, p. 76). He senses, however, that what is missing from this artificial memory can only be provided by a work which refuses to recognize its own artificiality – that is, a work of fiction. Of his analogies he says, "Ils n'auront pas pour venir rejoindre la parole présente dont la ressemblance les a attirés, à traverser la résistante douceur de cette atmosphère interposée qui a l'étendue même de notre vie et qui est toute la poésie de la mémoire" (*CSB*, p. 76n).

[7] Jessie Murray, "Marcel Proust as Critic and Disciple of Ruskin," *Nineteenth Century*, 101 (April 1927), p. 617.

[8] L. A. Bisson, "Proust and Ruskin Reconsidered in the Light of *Lettres à une amie*," *Modern Language Review*, 39 (Jan. 1944), 28-37.

[9] Chantal, II, 538.

[10] In a letter to Léon Bélugou, in *Robert de Montesquiou et Marcel Proust*, ed. Elisabeth de Clermont-Tonnerre (Paris: Flammarion, 1925), pp. 148-49; cited in Chantal, II, 547.

Chapter 2: The Magic Voyage: Proust Reads Nerval

[1] Benjamin, p. 359 (English text, p. 205).

[2] Benjamin, p. 356 (English text, p. 202).

[3] See, for example, Margaret Mein's chapter on Nerval in *A Foretaste of Proust: A Study of Proust and His Precursors* (New York: Atheneum, 1974) or the more general studies found in Chantal or Strauss.

[4] The fragmentary nature of *Contre Sainte-Beuve* is borne out by the disparity between the Bernard de Fallois edition (Paris: Gallimard, 1954), which included much fictional material later reworked into the *Recherche*, and the Clarac (Pléiade) edition (1970), which excluded all the fictional portions, but supplemented the critical essays from the *CSB*

notebooks with many other essays of Proust's criticism, such as the Ruskin essays. Unless otherwise noted, references here are to the Pléiade edition.

5 Clarac, in an introductory note, *CSB*, p. 820.

6 Terdiman, *The Dialectics of Isolation* (New Haven: Yale University Press, 1976), pp. 92-93.

7 Terdiman, p. 93.

8 From the Fallois edition of *Contre Sainte-Beuve*, p. 241; omitted from the Pléiade edition.

9 From the final part of Lemaitre's *Jean Racine* (Paris: Calmann-Lévy, 1908); cited by Clarac, *CSB*, p. 840n.

10 Flaubert, *Correspondance* (Paris: Conard, 1933-59), VII, 294; cited by Rousset to show Flaubert's concern for removing evidence of the writer and the act of writing from his work. Cf. "J'ai eu bien du ciment à enlever, qui bavachait entre les pierres, et il a fallu retasser les pierres, pour que les joints ne parussent pas" (*Correspondance*, III, 264); cited in Rousset, pp. 121-22.

11 I retain the use of the French *sincère* to distinguish Proust's concept from any moral category of sincerity.

12 From an early version of *Sylvie*, in *Œuvres*, ed. Albert Béguin and Jean Richer, Bibliothèque de la Pléiade, 5th ed. (Paris: Gallimard, 1974), I, 465.

Chapter 3: The Reader as Judge

1 One of the worst offenders is Proust's biographer, George Painter, whose extremely useful study nevertheless freely supplements the story of Proust's life with incidents from the novel.

2 Poulet, pp. 25-26.

3 Tadié, p. 272, referring to the following quotation: " . . . partir des illusions, des croyances qu'on rectifie peu à peu, comme Dostoïevsky raconterait une vie" (III, 983).

4 Deleuze, p. 7.

5 Faulkner has thematized this problem of "historical fiction" in *Absalom! Absalom!*, in which the story is told in an apparently omniscient voice, but by one of the characters. Quentin interrupts his narrative occasionally with a tentativeness which reveals him filling in gaps in the really sparse evidence available to him, while a nearly invisible narrator makes it clear that the reconstruction of events never goes beyond hypothesis: the whole remains a fictional continuity created between known points, a causal relationship interpolated between the parts.

6 Roger Shattuck, *Proust's Binoculars* (New York: Random House, 1963), p. 143. Doubrovsky (p. 98) also notes the deceptive function of the optical image in Proust.

7 Honoré de Balzac, "Les Secrets de la Princesse de Cadignan," in *La Comédie humaine*, ed. Pierre Citron, Edition l'Intégrale (Paris: Seuil, 1966), IV, 481.

8 Balzac, p. 481.

9 Balzac, p. 493.

Chapter 4: The Textuality of Albertine

1 The link between the writing project and the sexual project is not new. It has been explored in one aspect or another since Freud. Jacques Derrida even turned Freud upon himself, in his essay "La Scène de l'écriture," in *L'Ecriture et la différence* (Paris: Seuil, 1967). Doubrovsky, of course, also exploited this connection in Proust, even taking to an extreme the insights of Phillippe Lejeune's "Ecriture et sexualité," *Europe*, Nos. 502-03 (1971), pp. 113-43. My intention here is to focus on the similarity of desire to the reader's attempt to appropriate the text and on the characteristics of the text which make this similarity tenable.

2 Picon, p. 71.

3 From an early version of the *Recherche*, "Noms de personnes," in the Fallois edition of *Contre Sainte-Beuve*, pp. 268-69.

4 Fallois, p. 269.

5 Nerval, I, 242. Gérard later describes the moment when the visionary Aurélie becomes a realizable goal, "Je touchais du doigt mon idéal" (p. 244).

6 Poulet, p. 108.

7 Poulet, p. 109.

8 Marcel's attempt to seize the secret of the flow without sacrificing its essential movement is a project of comprehensive reading, not unlike the reader's attempt to grasp the movement of *A la recherche du temps perdu* itself, a project whose image we found in the carafes suspended in the Vivonne.

9 As when after Albertine escapes, Marcel only begins to suffer when Saint-Loup brings him details of her existence: "J'avais souffert une première fois quand s'était individualisé géographiquement le lieu où elle était, quand j'avais appris qu'au lieu d'être dans deux ou trois endroits possibles, elle était en Touraine" (III, 472). The particular seems to confront him inescapably with the real.

10 Bersani, *Marcel Proust: The Fictions of Life and Art* (New York: Oxford University Press, 1965), p. 59.

11 Poulet, p. 110.

12 Gide, p. 692. *Jean Santeuil*, with its transparent device of the "found" manuscript, can be seen as an early evasion of the first-person narrative. With the development of the fictional "je" in the *Recherche*, Proust is of course taking the procedure of "exculpating" the narrator one step further. The pseudo-autobiography, exploiting an apparent ingenuousness, is even more deceptive than a fictional third person—as Albertine is teaching Marcel.

13 For Proust, the Sodomites are by definition those who need to mask themselves, homosexuality and the heterosexual appearance being inseparable. He even plays on this connection describing their entry into Sodom: "Or, à peine arrivés, tous les Sodomites quitteraient la ville pour ne pas avoir l'air d'en être" (II, 632).

14 Moss, *The Magic Lantern of Marcel Proust* (London: Faber & Faber, 1963), p. 95.

Chapter 5: Marcel's Fictional Project: A Strategy of Recovery

1 Bersani, p. 199.

2 René Girard, *Mensonge romantique et vérité romanesque* (Paris: Grasset, 1961), p. 206.

3 In the essay "John Ruskin," Proust emphasized the individual nature of the sacred: "Seulement, quoique ce qui excite l'enthousiasme, ce qui commande le respect, ce qui provoque l'inspiration soit différent pour chacun, chacun finit par lui attribuer un caractère plus particulièrement sacré" *(CSB,* p. 112).

4 Butor, *Les Œuvres d'art imaginaires chez Proust* (London: Athalone Press, 1964), p. 38.

5 P. Zima has written a detailed sociohistorical account of the nobility's decline and the response of the bourgeoisie, *Le Désir du mythe* (Paris: Nizet, 1973). Despite its title, the book offers only a limited sense of the metaphorical implications of the "myth" of the nobility. For Zima, the nobility is important primarily as a figure of *political* power.

6 Bersani, p. 176.

7 Proust wrote to a friend, "Par la logique naturelle après avoir affronté à la poésie du lieu Balbec la banalité du pays Balbec, il me fallait procéder de même pour le nom de personne de Guermantes"–Proust, *Correspondance générale* (Paris: Plon, 1930-36), III, 305-06; cited in Tadié, p. 272. The repeated *reculements* resemble the loss of center noted earlier and the replacement of the missing object of desire by accessible intermediates. Without a sure point of departure, however, history is threatened: today's *parvenu* is tomorrow's old guard, cause is indistinguishable from effect, and one cannot know whether rank is the *cause* of a brilliant marriage or the result of it.

8 The language and experience here recall Marcel's encounter with "la dame en rose," the cocotte who shocks him by her diabolically ordinary appearance: "Et pourtant, en pensant à ce que devait être sa vie, l'immoralité m'en troublait peut-être plus que si elle avait été concrétisée devant moi en une apparence spéciale. . . . " (I, 77).

⁹ Barthes, *S/Z* (Paris: Seuil, 1970), esp. pp. 46-47. Balzac's story begins with the luxurious image of a family whose enormous wealth, and consequent social standing, arose from a Cardinal's affection for his favorite castrato singer.

Chapter 6: Conclusion: The Narrative Implications

¹ Jauss, p. 16.

² Flaubert, in a letter of 16 Jan. 1852, cited by Jauss, p. 14, and earlier, as he indicates, by Curtius (in *Französischer Geist im neuen Europa*). For both, Flaubert's statement is a declaration of independence from classical rules and traditions, yet Proust's transcendence of epic tradition (Jauss) can also be seen as part of the unsuccessful attempt to escape the materiality of language altogether.

³ David Mendelson, *Le Verre et les objets de verre dans l'univers imaginaire de Marcel Proust* (Paris: Corti, 1968), quoting from a fragmentary essay in *CSB*, p. 309.

⁴ This confusion may explain why Mendelson finds it necessary to rely on texts much earlier than the *Recherche*: Proust has reinscribed an earlier position of his own into the novel as Marcel's opinion.

⁵ Hartman, "Structuralism: The Anglo-American Adventure," in *Structuralism*, ed. Jacques Ehrmann (New York: Doubleday, 1970), p. 157.

⁶ Blanchot, *Le Livre à venir* (Paris: Gallimard, 1959), p. 33; Barthes, "Proust et les noms," p. 152; Benjamin, pp. 355-56 (English text, p. 202); Genette, *Figures* (I), p. 62. Earlier readers, such as Leo Spitzer, also noticed the complexity of the several "voices" in Proust's narrative, as "the nervousness of the reality-seeker" combined with a "sage-like calm"—"Zum Stil Marcel Prousts," in *Stilstudien II* (Munich: Hübner, 1928), p. 405.

⁷ The strategy recalls the attempt at mastery through repetition that Freud described, where a child masters the loneliness of his mother's absence by the "game" of making her "disappear"—*Beyond the Pleasure Principle*, trans. James Strachey (London: Hogarth, 1950), pp. 14-15.

⁸ The "horizontal" chronology of the nobility has of course already been stratified into the "vertical" hierarchy of the Faubourg.

⁹ As the anthropologist Marcel Mauss explained, the act of sacrifice is premised on the sanctification of its object: "Or en général, avant la cérémonie, ni le sacrifiant, ni le sacrificateur . . . n'ont ce caractère [religieux] au degré qui convient. La première phase du sacrifice a pour objet de le leur donner. Ils sont profanes; il faut qu'ils changent d'état. Pour cela, des rites sont nécessaires qui les introduisent dans le monde sacré. . . . C'est ce qui constitue, suivant l'expression même des textes sanscrits, *l'entrée dans le sacrifice*"—"L'Essai sur la nature et la fonction du sacrifice," in *Œuvres*, ed. V. Karady (Paris: Minuit, 1968), I, 212-13. Proust inscribes the reverse procedure into his novel, sacrificing *in order* to create the sacred.

¹⁰ Jauss, p. 32.

¹¹ Shattuck, *Proust* (London: Fontana, 1974), pp. 118f., and cf. Frank, *The Widening Gyre* (New Brunswick, N. J.: Rutgers University Press, 1963), pp. 24-25.

Bibliography

Works by Marcel Proust

A la recherche du temps perdu. Ed. Pierre Clarac and André Ferré. 3 vols. Bibliothèque de la Pléiade. Paris: Gallimard, 1954.

Chroniques. Paris: Gallimard, 1927.

Contre Sainte-Beuve: suivi de Nouveaux mélanges. Ed. with preface by Bernard de Fallois. Paris: Gallimard, 1954.

Contre Sainte-Beuve: précédé de Pastiches et mélanges et suivi de Essais et articles. Ed. Pierre Clarac and Yves Sandre. Bibliothèque de la Pléiade. Paris: Gallimard, 1971.

Jean Santeuil précédé de Les Plaisirs et les jours. Ed. Pierre Clarac and Yves Sandre. Bibliothèque de la Pléiade. Paris: Gallimard, 1971.

Textes retrouvés. Ed. Philip Kolb and Larkin Price. Urbana: University of Illinois Press, 1968.

Correspondence

Correspondance générale. 6 vols. Paris: Plon, 1930-36.

Autour de soixante lettres de Marcel Proust. Ed. Lucien Daudet. Paris: Gallimard, 1929.

Correspondance avec Mme Strauss. Ed. Suzy Mante-Proust. Paris: Plon, 1936.

Correspondance de Marcel Proust avec sa mère. Ed. Philip Kolb. Paris: Plon, 1953.

Lettres à André Gide. Neuchâtel-Paris: Ides et Calendes, 1949.

Lettres à la NRF. Paris: Gallimard, 1932.

Lettres à Reynaldo Hahn. Ed. Philip Kolb. Paris: Gallimard, 1956.

Marcel Proust et Jacques Rivière: Correspondance 1914-22. Ed. Philip Kolb. Paris: Plon, 1955.

Secondary Material

Autret, Jean. *L'Influence de Ruskin sur la vie, les idées et l'œuvre de Marcel Proust.* Geneva: Droz, 1955.

——, and William Buford. *On Reading.* New York: Macmillan, 1971.

Balzac, Honoré (de). *La Comédie humaine.* Ed. Pierre Citron. Edition l'Intégrale. Paris: Seuil, 1966.

Bardèche, Maurice. *Marcel Proust romancier.* 2 vols. Paris: Les Sept Couleurs, 1971.

Barthes, Roland. "Proust et les noms." In *To Honor Roman Jakobson.* The Hague: Mouton, 1967.

——. *S/Z.* Paris: Seuil, 1970.

Bell, William Stewart. *Proust's Nocturnal Muse.* New York: Columbia University Press, 1962.

Benjamin, Walter. *Illuminationen.* Ed. Siegfried Unseld. Frankfurt-am-Main: Suhrkamp, 1961. Trans. Harry Zohn as *Illuminations.* New York: Schocken, 1969.

Bersani, Leo. *Marcel Proust: The Fictions of Life and Art.* New York: Oxford University Press, 1965.

Bisson, L. A. "Proust and Ruskin: Reconsidered in the Light of *Lettres à une amie.*" *Modern Language Review*, 39 (Jan. 1944), 28-37.

Black, Carl, Jr. "Albertine as an Allegorical Figure of Time." *Romanic Review*, 54 (Oct. 1963), 171-86.

Blanchot, Maurice. *Le Livre à venir.* Paris: Gallimard, 1959.

Bonnet, Henri. *Marcel Proust de 1907 à 1914.* Paris: Nizet, 1971.

Bornecque, Jacques-Henri. *Un autre Proust.* Paris: Nizet, 1976.

Brée, Germaine. *Du temps perdu au temps retrouvé.* Paris: Belles Lettres, 1950. Trans. C. J. Richards and A. D. Truitt as *Marcel Proust and Deliverance from Time.* New Brunswick, N. J.: Rutgers University Press, 1955.

——. *The World of Marcel Proust.* London: Chatto and Windus, 1967.

Bucknall, Barbara. *The Religion of Art in Proust.* Urbana: University of Illinois Press, 1970.

Butor, Michel. *Les Œuvres d'art imaginaires chez Proust.* London: Athalone Press, 1964.

Chantal, René de. *Marcel Proust: Critique littéraire.* 2 vols. Montreal: University of Montreal Press, 1967.

Bibliography

Cocking, John M. *Proust*. London: Bowes and Bowes, 1956.

Crosman, Inge. "Metaphorical Function in *A la recherche du temps perdu*." *Romanic Review*, 67 (1976), 290-99.

Curtius, Ernst R. "Marcel Proust." In *Französischer Geist im zwanzigsten Jahrhundert*. Bern: Francke, 1952.

Deleuze, Gilles. *Marcel Proust et les signes*. Paris: P. U. F., 1970.

De Man, Paul. " 'New criticism' et nouvelle critique." *Preuves*, No. 188 (Oct. 1966), pp. 29-37.

―――. "Proust et l'allégorie de la lecture." In *Mouvements premiers: Etudes critiques offertes à Georges Poulet*. Paris: Corti, 1972.

Derrida, Jacques. *De la grammatologie*. Paris: Minuit, 1967.

―――. *L'Ecriture et la différence*. Paris: Seuil, 1967.

Doubrovsky, Serge. *La Place de la madeleine: Ecriture et fantasme chez Proust*. Paris: Mercure de France, 1974.

Ehrmann, Jacques, ed. *Structuralism*. New York: Doubleday, 1970.

Festa-McCormick, Diane. "Proustian Aesthetics of Ambiguity: Elstir's 'Miss Sacripant.' " *International Fiction Review*, 3 (1976), 92-99.

Feuillerat, Albert. *Comment Marcel Proust a composé son roman*. New Haven: Yale University Press, 1934.

Frank, Joseph. *The Widening Gyre: Crisis and Mastery in Modern Literature*. New Brunswick, N. J.: Rutgers University Press, 1963.

Freud, Sigmund. *Beyond the Pleasure Principle*. Trans. and ed. James Strachey. London: Hogarth Press, 1950.

―――. *Collected Papers*. Ed. Ernest Jones. Trans. Joan Rivière. 4 vols. London: Hogarth Press, 1950.

Genette, Gérard. *Figures* (I). Paris: Seuil, 1966.

―――. *Figures II*. Paris: Seuil, 1969.

―――. *Figures III*. Paris: Seuil, 1972.

Girard, René. *Mensonge romantique et vérité romanesque*. Paris: Grasset, 1961.

―――. *La Violence et le sacré*. Paris: Grasset, 1972.

Graham, Victor E. *The Imagery of Proust*. Oxford: Blackwell, 1966.

Green, F. C. *The Mind of Proust*. Cambridge: At the University Press, 1949.

Gutwirth, Marcel. "Le Portrait de Charlus dans l'œuvre de Proust." *Romanic Review*, 40 (Oct. 1949), 180-85.

Harlow, Barbara. "Sur la lecture." *Modern Language Notes*, 90 (1975), 849-71.

Hindus, Milton. *The Proustian Vision*. New York: Columbia University Press, 1953.

Hjelmslev, Louis. *Prolegomena to a Theory of Language*. Trans. F. J. Whitfield. 2nd ed. Madison: University of Wisconsin Press, 1963.

Iser, Wolfgang. *Der implizite Leser*. Munich: Fink, 1972.

Jauss, Hans-Robert. *Zeit und Erinnerung in Marcel Prousts "A la recherche du temps perdu": ein Beitrag zur Theorie des Romans*. Heidelberg: Carl Winter Verlag, 1955.

———, ed. *Poetik und Hermeneutik I: Nachahmung und Illusion*. Munich: Fink, 1964.

Köhler, Erich. *Marcel Proust*. Göttingen: Vandenhoeck and Ruprecht, 1967.

Kolb, Philip. "An Enigmatic Proustian Metaphor." *Romanic Review*, 54 (Oct. 1963), 187-97.

Lapp, John. "Proust's Windows to Reality." *Romanic Review*, 67 (1976), 38-49.

Lejeune, Phillipe. "Ecriture et sexualité." *Europe*, Nos. 502-03 (1971), pp. 113-43.

———. "Les Carafes de la Vivonne." *Poétique*, No. 31 (1977), pp. 285-305.

Lemaître, Henri. *Proust et Ruskin*. Toulouse: Privat-Didier, 1944.

Lévi-Strauss, Claude. *Mythologiques I: Le Cru et le cuit*. Paris: Plon, 1964.

———. *La Pensée sauvage*. Paris: Plon, 1962.

Levin, Harry. "Proust et Balzac." *Hommage à Balzac*. Paris: Mercure de France, 1950.

———. "Proust, Gide and the Sexes." *PMLA*, 65 (June 1950), 648-52.

Linn, John G. "Notes on Proust's Manipulation of Chronology." *Romanic Review*, 52 (Oct. 1961), 210-25.

———. "Proust's Theatrical Metaphors." *Romanic Review*, 49 (Oct. 1958), 179-90.

———. *The Theater in the Fiction of Marcel Proust*. Athens, Ohio: Ohio University Press, 1966.

Martin-Chauffier, Louis. "Proust ou le double 'je' des quatre personnages." *Confluences*, 1943. Reprinted in shorter form in English as "Proust and the Double 'I.'" *Partisan Review*, 16 (Oct. 1949), 1011-26.

Maurois, André. *A la recherche de Marcel Proust*. Paris: Hachette, 1949.

Mauss, Marcel. *Œuvres*. Ed. Victor Karady. 3 vols. Paris: Minuit, 1968.

Mehlman, Jeffrey, ed. *French Freud. Yale French Studies*, No. 48 (1972).

Mein, Margaret. *A Foretaste of Proust: A Study of Proust and His Precursors*. New York: Atheneum, 1974.

Mendelson, David. *Le Verre et les objets de verre dans l'univers imaginaire de Marcel Proust*. Paris: Corti, 1968.

Milly, Jean. *La Phrase de Proust*. Paris: Larousse, 1976.

Moss, Howard. *The Magic Lantern of Marcel Proust*. London: Faber & Faber, 1963.

Mouton, Jean. *Le Style de Marcel Proust*. Paris: Corréa, 1948.

Müller, Marcel. *Les Voix narratives dans "La Recherche du temps perdu."* Geneva: Droz, 1965.

Murray, Jessie. "Marcel Proust as a Critic and Disciple of Ruskin." *Nineteenth Century*, 101 (April 1927), 614-19.

Nerval, Gérard de. *Œuvres*. Ed. Albert Béguin and Jean Richer. Bibliothèque de la Pléiade. 5th ed. 2 vols. Paris: Gallimard, 1974.

O'Brien, Justin. "Albertine the Ambiguous: Notes on Proust's Transposition of the Sexes." *PMLA*, 64 (Dec. 1949), 933-52.

Pabst, Walter, and L. Schrader, ed. *"L'Affaire Lemoine" von Marcel Proust: Kommentare und Interpretationen*. Berlin: Erich Schmidt, 1972.

Painter, George. *Marcel Proust: A Biography*. 2 vols. London: Chatto and Windus, 1959 and 1965.

Pasco, Allan. "Albertine's Equivocal Eyes." *Australian Journal of French Studies*, 5 (1968), 257-62.

―――. *The Color-Keys to "A la recherche du temps perdu."* Geneva: Droz, 1976.

―――. "Proust's Reader and the Voyage of Self-Discovery." *Contemporary Literature*, 13 (1977), 20-37.

Peirce, Charles. *The Philosophy of Peirce*. Ed. Justus Buchler. London: K. Paul, Trench, Trubner, 1940.

Picon, Gaëtan. *Lecture de Proust*. Paris: Mercure de France, 1963.

Poulet, Georges. *L'Espace proustien*. Paris: Gallimard, 1963.

―――. *Etudes sur le temps humain*. Paris: Plon, 1950.

Poulet, Georges. *Mesure de l'instant*. Paris: Plon, 1968.

———. *Trois essais de mythologie romantique*. Paris: Corti, 1966.

Richard, Jean-Pierre. *Proust et le monde sensible*. Paris: Seuil, 1974.

Rogers, B. G. *Proust's Narrative Techniques*. Geneva: Droz, 1965.

Rososco, Joan. "Aux sources de la Vivonne." *Poétique*, No. 25 (1976), pp. 72-85.

Rousset, Jean. *Forme et signification*. Paris: Corti, 1962.

Ruskin, John. *The Works of John Ruskin*. Ed. E. T. Cook and A. Wedderburn. 38 vols. London: G. Allen, 1903-12.

Said, Edward. *Beginnings: Intention and Method*. New York: Basic Books, 1975.

Schlegel, Friedrich. *Kritische Schriften*. Ed. W. Rasch. Munich: Hanser, 1956.

Shattuck, Roger. *Proust's Binoculars: A Study of Memory, Time and Recognition in "A la recherche du temps perdu."* New York: Random House, 1963.

———. *Proust*. Modern Masters Series. London: Fontana, 1974.

Souza, Sybil de. *L'Influence de Ruskin sur Proust*. Montpellier: Manufacture de la charité, 1932.

Spitzer, Leo. *Stilstudien II: Stilsprachen*. Munich: Hübner, 1928.

Stambolian, George. *Marcel Proust and the Creative Encounter*. Chicago: University of Chicago Press, 1972.

Stierle, Karlheinz. *Dunkelheit und Form in Gérard de Nerval's "Chimères."* Munich: Fink, 1967.

———. "L'Histoire comme exemple, l'exemple comme histoire." *Poétique*, No. 10 (1972), pp. 176-98.

Strauss, Walter. *Proust and Literature: The Novelist as Critic*. Cambridge: Harvard University Press, 1957.

Sullivan, Dennis G. "On Theatricality in Proust." *Modern Language Notes*, 86 (May 1971), 532-54.

Suzuki, Michihiko. "Le 'je' proustien." *Bulletin de la Société des Amis de Marcel Proust*, 9 (1959), 69-82.

Tadié, Jean-Yves. "Invention d'un langage." *Nouvelle revue française*, 81 (Sept. 1959), 500-13.

———. *Lecture de Proust*. Paris: Colin, 1971.

Tadié, Jean-Yves. "Proust et le 'nouvel écrivain.' " *Revue d'Histoire littéraire de la France*, 67 (March 1967), 79-81.

──────. *Proust et le roman: Essai sur les formes et techniques du roman dans "A la recherche du temps perdu."* Paris: Gallimard, 1971.

Terdiman, Richard. *The Dialectics of Isolation.* New Haven: Yale University Press, 1976.

Trilling, Lionel. *The Liberal Imagination.* New York: Viking, 1950.

Ullmann, Stephen. *The Image in the Modern French Novel.* Cambridge: At the University Press, 1960.

──────. *Style in the French Novel.* Cambridge: At the University Press, 1957.

Valéry, Paul. *Œuvres.* Ed. Jean Hytier. Bibliothèque de la Pléiade. Paris: Gallimard, 1959.

Warning, Rainer, ed. *Rezeptionsästhetik.* Munich: Fink, 1975.

Waters, Harold. "The Narrator, not Marcel." *French Review*, 33 (Feb. 1960), 389-92.

Zima, P. *Le Désir du mythe: Une lecture sociologique de Marcel Proust.* Paris: Nizet, 1973.